The Magic of Mycology

An Enthusiast's Guide to Cultivating and Understanding Psilocybin Mushrooms

Chris J. Conlan

Exclusive Invitation Inside: Simplify Your Psilocybin Cultivation Journey

As an insightful reader of "The Magic of Mycology," you've embarked on a captivating journey into the world of psilocybin mushrooms. Ready to take your knowledge and skills to the next level?

We present to you "Psilocybin Simplified: A Rapid Guide to Mushroom Cultivation and Microdose Capsule Making." This guide is your practical roadmap to mastering the art of growing psilocybin mushrooms and preparing microdose capsules. It's packed with straightforward, step-by-step instructions tailored for enthusiasts seeking simplicity and clarity in their cultivation practice.

Picture yourself confidently cultivating your own psilocybin mushrooms with ease, creating accurate microdoses, and accessing a world of mycological resources. "Psilocybin Simplified" is designed to transform complex processes into an accessible, easy-to-follow guide. It's more than just a manual; it's your key to unlocking a rewarding and successful mycological experience.

To access your free copy of "Psilocybin Simplified," simply visit magicofmycology.com and enter your email address. Join a community of like-minded mycology enthusiasts and start your journey towards effortless mushroom cultivation and microdosing today.

Don't wait to enhance your mycological pursuits. Visit magicofmycology.com, grab your free guide, and step into a world where growing psilocybin mushrooms is simplified, just for you.

Contents

Introduction

In a dimly lit room, the soft cadence of music emanates from the corner, setting the stage for an extraordinary journey. A small group gathers, anticipation in their eyes, as they prepare to embark on a path of exploration, healing, and discovery. On the table is a collection of unassuming mushrooms—objects of curiosity, reverence, fear, and misunderstanding. This is the world of psilocybin, a substance both ancient and modern, both mystical and scientific.

It is said that the keys to the universe lie in things so small that we often overlook them. Psilocybin, the psychedelic compound found in over 180 species of mushrooms, might just hold one of those keys. Its potential to unlock the human mind, heal mental afflictions, and provide profound insights into the nature of consciousness has placed it at the forefront of a vibrant and evolving conversation.

Psilocybin, the active compound in psychedelic mushrooms, is a molecule that has captured the human imagination for centuries. It is a serendipitous natural concoction that can unlock doors of perception, offering glimpses into the unexplored corridors of the mind.

The journey of psilocybin is one that transcends cultures, laws, and even the boundaries of our own minds. Its story is interwoven with the very fabric of human history, from the sacred rituals of indigenous tribes to the cutting-edge laboratories of contemporary scientists.

Fast forward to the 20th century, psilocybin mushrooms have found themselves at the heart of the psychedelic movement. Pioneers like Timothy Leary and Terence McKenna sang praises of their potential to break down societal barriers, enhance creativity, and foster deep personal insights.

Recent studies have highlighted the therapeutic potential of psilocybin, from treating conditions like depression, anxiety, PTSD, and addiction to unlocking doors of consciousness and creativity. The present-day analysis has added layers of credibility and acceptance to what was once considered purely recreational or mystical.

The legal journey of psilocybin is a maze. Different countries, even different states within countries, have wildly varying laws, reflecting societal attitudes and the political climate. Whether you find yourself in the liberal landscape of Canada or the more stringent regions of other nations, the legal status of psilocybin is a complex and nuanced issue.

Recent years have seen a wave of decriminalization as awareness grows of psilocybin's potential benefits. Movements are rising, debates are flourishing, and in some places, the laws are changing. From Oregon to Denver, a new era is dawning where psilocybin might be accepted and regulated rather than feared and banned.

Introduction

In this book, we will embark on a voyage that uncovers the mysteries of psilocybin. We'll explore the therapeutic benefits, delving into current medical and psychological research, analyzing its potential effects on consciousness and creativity, and reflecting on its place in future medical treatments.

It's a journey that requires an open mind and a willing heart. As we navigate the winding paths of understanding, we may discover that the enigmatic world of psilocybin is not just a story of a substance, but a reflection of ourselves, our society, and our unending quest for healing and understanding.

Join me as we embark on this thrilling and enlightening journey together. The door is open, the path is clear, and the mysteries of psilocybin await. The enigmatic world of psilocybin offers a profound and multifaceted story that reaches into the depths of human history, psychology, law, and culture. This book aims to unravel those threads, providing an in-depth exploration of a subject that has fascinated, confused, and inspired humanity for generations.

With insights drawn from history, science, law, and personal experience, we will explore the potential of this small yet mighty molecule to influence our lives in profound and lasting ways. Whether you come to this subject with curiosity, skepticism, or personal interest, there is a place for you on this journey. Together, we will explore the potential of psilocybin to heal, enlighten, and transform our world.

Chapter 1
A Brief History of Psilocybin Mushrooms

Imagine for a moment, walking through a dense forest after a refreshing bout of rain. The earthy aroma envelops you, and as you glance down, you spot a multitude of mushrooms sprouting amid the fallen leaves. Now, think back to our ancestors, millennia ago, wandering through similar forests, driven by hunger, curiosity, or spiritual inquiry. It's in these forests that they might have stumbled upon a unique kind of mushroom, one that, when consumed, transported them to realms beyond ordinary comprehension.

Our journey with fungi goes way back—these organisms played pivotal roles in our ecosystem, aiding decomposition and nutrient cycling long before humans walked the earth. Yet, as we evolved, so did our relationship with them. The early humans' encounters with fungi were multifaceted: They provided sustenance, remedies for ailments, and, yes, potential threats. Among these fungal finds, psilocybin mushrooms held a particular allure, prompting speculation that our ancestors might have chanced upon their transcendent powers.

If you deep dive into history, you'll find clues of these "magic mushrooms" being revered. In the relics of Central and South American cultures, you'll find tales told not in words but in stone—the mysterious "mushroom stones." These artifacts whisper of ancient ceremonies, where psilocybin might have been a conduit to the divine, linking shamans and their deities. Fast forward a few millennia and the 20th century saw a renewed intrigue in these mystical fungi. From R. Gordon Wasson's evocative experiences in the heart of Mexico to Albert Hofmann's groundbreaking isolation of psilocybin, the scientific community began to take note.

But, as with any potent force, the rise of psychedelics in the 1960s was a double-edged sword. While they burgeoned as tools of enlightenment and rebellion against the establishment, society's cogs began to resist. The media's portrayal, a growing moral panic, and stringent legal measures saw psychedelics, including psilocybin, shunned into obscurity. Yet, like the phoenix, interest in these enigmatic mushrooms is seeing a spirited resurgence in the 21st century. Scientists, therapists, and enthusiasts alike are heralding the "psychedelic renaissance" as they unravel the potential of psilocybin in treating conditions that ail the modern mind.

So, as we embark on this journey together, delving into the annals of history and emerging scientific endeavors, let's unravel the story of psilocybin mushrooms—a tale as old as time yet as relevant as tomorrow.

The Role of Fungi in Early Human History

From the early days of our species, fungi have sparked human interest. Hunter-gatherer societies likely stumbled upon different fungi types in their foraging endeavors. These encounters would have been a trial-and-error process: Some fungi were nutritious and tasty, becoming part of the regular diet. Others held medicinal attributes, useful in treating wounds or illnesses. Still, others revealed themselves to be dangerous or even lethal.

This relationship, anchored in both admiration and caution, set the stage for fungi's cultural, spiritual, and medicinal roles in various societies. Shamans and healers would have noticed the powerful effects of some mushrooms, incorporating them into rituals and treatments.

Ancient Uses of Psilocybin in Religious and Spiritual Rituals

The mysticism and allure of psychedelics, specifically psilocybin-containing mushrooms, have captured human imagination and curiosity for millennia. Ancient cultures and civilizations, from Central and South America to the remote corners of the world, have embraced the spiritual significance of these fungi. This extensive essay delves into the ancient use of psilocybin in religious and spiritual rituals, touching on evidence from Central and South American cultures, exploring the enigmatic "mushroom stones," and theorizing about its role in ancient religious and shamanic practices (Strauss et al., 2023).

Evidence of Psilocybin Use in Central and South American Cultures

Central and South America stand as significant centers for the ancient use of psychedelics. Various Indigenous tribes and high civilizations, such as the Aztecs and Mayans, have historically revered psilocybin mushrooms as sacred instruments for communion with deities, spirits, and ancestors.

For instance, the Aztecs referred to psilocybin mushrooms as teonanácatl, which can be translated to "god's flesh." Consumed during religious ceremonies and spiritual gatherings, these mushrooms were believed to open portals to the divine and the supernatural. Aztec priests and shamans would consume them to communicate with gods and receive guidance on governance, warfare, and agriculture (Oana-Mihaela, n.d.).

In South America, tribes in the Amazon basin have been found to use a diverse array of psychoactive substances, including plants and fungi, for shamanic rituals. The powerful brew, ayahuasca, often overshadows psilocybin in discourse, but ancient rock art and oral traditions hint at the sacred status of the mushroom.

The "Mushroom Stones" and Other Archaeological Finds

Among the most intriguing archaeological evidence of ancient psilocybin use are the "mushroom stones" discovered primarily in the Guatemalan highlands and Mexico. These stone carvings, dating back to 1000–500 BCE, depict humanoids or deities with mushroom caps, suggesting a ritualistic or divine association.

Beyond sculptures, ancient murals—like those found in the Temple of the Murals in Bonampak, Mexico—display scenes of mushroom consumption. These vivid illustrations provide compelling evidence of the mushrooms' integration into spiritual rites and ceremonies.

Theories About the Role of Psilocybin in Ancient Religious and Shamanic Practices

Exploring the research of Michael James Winkelman on shamanism, coupled with the developed psychology of psychedelic ambiance and preparation, offers an extensive perspective on psilocybin's function in age-old civilizations. As Winkelman explains, shamanism is an integral part of our psychological evolution, stemming from long-standing community demonstrations and intentional changes in awareness through rituals and inherent recuperative reactions (Winkelman, 2021).

Shamanism and Evolutionary Psychology

The psychedelic properties of psilocybin enhance innate cognitive faculties like self-awareness, "mind reading," and spatial intelligence. These traits are also core features of shamanism. Given the evolutionary links between humans and psilocybin-containing fungi, it's plausible to believe that psychedelics could have influenced our ancestors' spiritual practices. Shamanic settings were often communal, highlighted by singing, drumming, and dancing—all of which are reminiscent of the effects of psychedelics.

This bond between psychedelics and evolutionary psychology posits that humans developed specific orientations to optimally harness the natural properties of these substances. The collective and shared experiences induced by psychedelics might have paved the way for the establishment of cultural norms, values, and beliefs, grounding societies in shared realities.

Chris J. Conlan

Integration of Shamanic Practices and Psilocybin Use

Ancient shamans were revered figures, intermediaries between the physical and spiritual realms. Through the consumption of psilocybin mushrooms, they would enter altered states of consciousness, embarking on soul flights, experiencing death and rebirth, and communing with spirits.

Psilocybin, as an exogenous neurotransmitter analog, likely played a pivotal role in the evolution of human sociability. The interconnectedness felt during psychedelic experiences could have fostered group cohesion, empathy, and collective well-being. Thus, the rituals and ceremonies centered around these mushrooms became fundamental in building and maintaining social harmony.

The enigmatic relationship between humans and psilocybin has roots buried deep within ancient civilizations, from the bustling metropolises of the Aztecs to the remote tribes of the Amazon. These mushrooms were not mere recreational tools but were divine conduits, facilitating communion with the metaphysical.

Today, as modern science revisits the therapeutic potentials of psychedelics, it's imperative to acknowledge and respect the profound wisdom and understanding of our ancestors. Their rituals, ceremonies, and beliefs surrounding psilocybin offer invaluable insights, guiding us toward a harmonious integration of these ancient tools into contemporary society.

Early 20th Century Studies and Encounters With Psilocybin

The early 20th century bore witness to a whirlwind of exploration and discovery. Among the tales of far-off lands and long-forgotten rituals, psilocybin, a naturally occurring psychedelic compound in magic mushrooms, stood as one of the most enthralling mysteries. Though humans had consumed it for over 10,000 years, its reintroduction to modern consciousness during this era would reshape our understanding of psychedelics, spiritual ceremonies, and, in many ways, the mind itself.

R. Gordon Wasson's Encounters With Psilocybin in Mexico

R. Gordon Wasson, an amateur ethnomycologist and Vice President at J.P. Morgan, stood as a pivotal figure in the reawakening of interest in magic mushrooms in the 20th century (Garcia de Teresa, 2022). With an insatiable appetite for adventure, Wasson and his wife, Valentina, had already spent three decades traversing the world, documenting varying cultural attitudes toward wild mushrooms. Their quest wasn't purely academic; they were immersing themselves in the folk legacies—the whispered tales passed down through generations. Wasson wasn't as fascinated by what scholars knew about mushrooms than by the untold stories and practices of unassuming villagers and country folk.

It was on a fateful day in 1955 that Wasson's journey took a dramatic turn. With a photographer in tow, he made his way to the Mazatec region in Mexico. There, in a simple mud hut, he met María Sabina, a revered Mazatec curandera (medicine woman). Little did he know that this encounter would forever change the course of psychedelic history. Wasson and his companion had the distinction of becoming, in his words, the "first white men in recorded history to eat the divine mushrooms" (Partridge, 2018).

This profound experience compelled Wasson to pen an article titled "Seeking the Magic Mushroom" for Life magazine in 1957. This narrative wasn't just an account; it was a revelation for many. While it ignited the flame of the American psychedelic counterculture, it also inadvertently led to the defilement of sacred mushroom rituals and a surge in unwarranted attention on María Sabina. For better or worse, the lid had been lifted off Pandora's Box.

The Discovery and Isolation of Psilocybin by Albert Hofmann

Parallel to Wasson's ethnomycological pursuits, a brilliant Swiss chemist named Albert Hofmann was making groundbreaking strides in the scientific arena. Hofmann, already famed for synthesizing the psychedelic compound LSD from ergot in 1938, was no stranger to the mysteries of mind-altering substances.

While Wasson's pursuits were ethnographic, Hofmann's were purely scientific. By the late 1950s, Hofmann had heard of the psychedelic effects of the Psilocybe mexicana mushrooms, largely due to Wasson's accounts. Intrigued, he obtained samples from an amateur mycologist. With meticulous precision, in 1958, Hofmann isolated and then synthesized the primary hallucinogenic compounds from these mushrooms: psilocybin and psilocin. This groundbreaking discovery demystified the active ingredients behind the age-old Mazatec rituals.

Hofmann's extensive research in psychedelics wasn't just a chemist's curiosity. Deeply captivated by the effects and potential therapeutic applications of these substances, he believed that, under controlled circumstances, they could serve as powerful tools for psychiatric treatment. His pioneering work paved the way for a surge of scientific interest in the properties and potential of psilocybin and other psychedelics.

Early Scientific and Medical Interest in Psilocybin's Effects

The mid-20th century was a time of burgeoning curiosity. With Wasson's firsthand accounts capturing the public's imagination and Hofmann's scientific endeavors validating the psychedelic properties of psilocybin, the compound drew immense interest.

The promise of psilocybin was manifold. Hofmann's initial encounters with LSD had already hinted at the therapeutic potential of psychedelics. Psilocybin appeared as another key in potentially unlocking the secrets of the human psyche. Early researchers conjectured its potential in treating various mental health disorders, especially given Hofmann's own exploration of its effects and his unwavering belief in its therapeutic potential.

Yet, as with many groundbreaking discoveries, the allure of psilocybin was a double-edged sword. The same fascination that drove scientists and medical professionals to explore its potential therapeutic uses also lured recreational users and those seeking spiritual enlightenment. This dichotomy would, over time, result in contentious debates, regulatory crackdowns, and, for a period, the sidelining of psilocybin from mainstream research.

The early 20th century's explorations and discoveries around psilocybin were a confluence of serendipity, cultural intrigue, and scientific prowess. Figures like R. Gordon Wasson and Albert Hofmann not only pioneered our modern understanding of psilocybin but also beckoned us to question the nature of consciousness, spirituality, and therapeutic interventions. As the world danced to the tunes of a changing era, psilocybin stood as a testament to humanity's eternal quest for understanding, healing, and transcendence.

The Impact and Backlash of the Rise of Psychedelics in the Mid-20th Century

As the 20th century reached its mid-point, society sat on the brink of profound transformation. One of the most defining aspects of this era was the rise of psychedelics—substances that would push boundaries, reshape cultures, and inspire both awe and fear. Amid this upheaval, psilocybin, a psychedelic compound found in magic mushrooms, emerged as an emblem of change, freedom, and rebellion.

Psilocybin and the Counterculture Movement of the 1960s

The 1960s heralded a decade of questioning authority, pushing social boundaries, and seeking new forms of consciousness. As youth around the world began to voice their dissatisfaction with established norms and societal constraints, they sought new experiences and avenues of expression. Psilocybin, with its capacity to alter perceptions and open the mind to uncharted realms, fits perfectly within this paradigm.

The psychedelic experiences triggered by psilocybin were not just hedonistic escapades; they were seen as a means to connect deeper with oneself and the universe, breaking free from the shackles of conventionality. The counterculture, thirsty for change, embraced psilocybin as both a tool and symbol of their revolution against the status quo.

Music festivals, art installations, and even spontaneous gatherings in parks and forests became hotspots for psilocybin consumption. The substance, along with others like LSD, became synonymous with the hippie movement, Woodstock, and the Summer of Love. Lyrics from iconic bands like The Beatles and The Grateful Dead resonated with references to these substances and the experiences they induced.

Timothy Leary and the Harvard Psilocybin Project

No discussion on psychedelics in the 20th century would be complete without mentioning Dr. Timothy Leary, a charismatic Harvard psychologist. Leary was initially a respectable academic with a keen interest in behavioral change. However, a series of personal encounters with psilocybin and other psychedelics shifted his trajectory dramatically.

In 1960, Leary initiated the Harvard Psilocybin Project along with Dr. Richard Alpert (later known as Ram Dass) (Witt, 2018). Their aim was not mere curiosity; they believed psychedelics held the key to profound therapeutic benefits. The project involved guided sessions where participants, including graduate students, ingested psilocybin to explore its effects on human consciousness.

Leary's famous mantra, "Turn on, tune in, drop out," encapsulated the ethos of the era. He advocated for the widespread use of psychedelics, not just as recreational substances, but as catalysts for profound personal and societal transformation (Bach et al., 2013).

However, Leary's methods, along with his increasingly public endorsement of widespread psychedelic use, attracted scrutiny. Concerns began to rise about the safety and ethics of administering these potent substances without stringent controls. By 1963, amid growing controversy, Harvard University severed its ties with both Leary and the Psilocybin Project.

The Backlash

The wave of enthusiasm for psilocybin and other psychedelics eventually met a tidal wave of opposition. As reports of bad trips, accidents, and mental health issues related to unsupervised psychedelic use began to surface, the media took note.

Newspapers and television programs began running stories portraying psychedelics as dangerous, mind-destroying drugs. Tales of young people losing their sanity, jumping off buildings believing they could fly, or spiraling into psychosis began to circulate. While some of these stories had a basis in truth, many were sensationalized or taken out of context, further fueling the growing moral panic.

The political establishment, too, took a stern view of the burgeoning psychedelic movement. Authorities were wary of the anti-establishment sentiments being echoed by the counterculture, and the association of psychedelics with these sentiments made them a target. Psilocybin, despite its ancient history and recent scientific exploration, was caught in the crosshairs.

The legal clampdown began in the late 1960s and early 1970s. Countries around the world, led by the United States, started criminalizing the possession, sale, and consumption of psilocybin and other psychedelics. These substances were not only deemed illegal but were categorized alongside some of the most dangerous narcotics, with hefty penalties for those caught in their possession.

The narrative around psychedelics, including psilocybin, underwent a radical shift. From substances that promised personal enlightenment and societal revolution, they were now broadly viewed as dangerous, mind-warping drugs. The research that had once promised to unlock their therapeutic potential was stifled as funding dried up and the legal noose tightened.

The Psychedelic Renaissance

Ancient civilizations revered psilocybin-containing mush-rooms for their spiritual and medicinal properties. Yet, the modern narrative took a dramatic shift in the mid-20th century. Stigmatization, cultural perceptions, and legal restric-tions suppressed and hindered research on this profound compound. Fast forward to the 21st century, and we find ourselves amid a "psychedelic renaissance." This era signifies an awakening—a revival of interest in the untapped potential of psychedelics like psilocybin.

The 1960s and 1970s psychedelic counterculture movements often painted these substances as recreational and escapist.

However, this modern resurgence steers the conversation toward their medical, therapeutic, and transformative potentials. The scientific community, in particular, has placed a magnifying glass over psilocybin and its potential applications.

Landmark Studies on the Medical Potential of Psilocybin

Depression, Anxiety, and End-of-Life Care

While pharmaceuticals like selective serotonin reuptake inhibitors (SSRIs) have been the primary treatment for mood disorders like depression and anxiety, they are not always effective for all patients. Moreover, they can come with a slew of side effects. Psilocybin, as emerging studies suggest, might offer an alternative.

Clinical trials have illuminated psilocybin's profound effects on patients with treatment-resistant depression. Participants reported significant reductions in symptoms compared to placebo groups. In some studies, the efficacy of psilocybin mirrored or even surpassed that of conventional SSRIs, suggesting its potential as a formidable contender in treating mood disorders.

Beyond its direct medicinal potential, psilocybin also holds promise for those in the end-of-life phase. Individuals diagnosed with terminal illnesses often face profound existential distress, grappling with questions of meaning, purpose, and mortality. Preliminary studies have shown that a single, carefully supervised psilocybin session can offer relief from these end-of-life psychological crises. Many patients describe a shift in perspective, feeling more connected to the world and less fearful of death.

Addiction

The labyrinth of addiction has always been challenging to navigate, both for those trapped within it and for those trying to help. Traditional therapies have seen varied success, but addiction, in many cases, remains a formidable adversary.

Enter psilocybin. Studies, albeit in their infancy, have begun to suggest that this psychedelic compound might be a game-changer. Trials focusing on nicotine and alcohol addiction have showcased psilocybin's potential superiority over existing treatments. The mechanisms are still under investigation, but many believe that the profound, introspective experiences induced by psilocybin may facilitate a cognitive "reset," allowing individuals to break free from the chains of addiction.

Changes in Legal and Social Attitudes

As scientific research piles up in favor of psychedelics, societal attitudes have started to shift. Once demonized and relegated to the fringes, compounds like psilocybin are gradually moving into the limelight, garnering interest and acceptance.

Legal frameworks are evolving. Recognizing the medicinal potential and low risk of overuse and toxicity, some jurisdictions are reevaluating their stance on psilocybin. Decriminalization movements are gaining traction, and in some places, medical exemptions have been carved out for their therapeutic use.

The broader public is also displaying increased openness. As the benefits of psychedelics seep into public consciousness, there is a growing acceptance and curiosity. Books, documentaries, and advocacy campaigns are changing the narrative, highlighting not just the recreational but the therapeutic and transformative potential of these compounds.

The 21st century has witnessed a groundbreaking shift in the understanding and appreciation of psychedelics. As we continue to delve deeper into the mysteries of the mind and the potential of compounds like psilocybin, we stand at the cusp of a new era in mental health treatment. An era that beckons with promise, not just for healing but for transformation. This psychedelic renaissance, rooted in ancient wisdom and propelled by modern science, offers a beacon of hope for countless individuals seeking relief, meaning, and connection in a rapidly changing world.

Conclusion

From the enigmatic fungi that have been integral to the ecosystem since time immemorial to their deep-seated ties with early human civilizations, psilocybin mushrooms have woven a rich tapestry of interaction with our species. Their ancient significance in spiritual and shamanic rituals is immortalized in relics like Central America's "mushroom stones," hinting at profound mystical experiences. As the 20th century dawned, figures like R. Gordon Wasson and Albert Hofmann heralded a scientific exploration of these entheogens, culminating in the psychedelic fervor of the 1960s. However, the ensuing societal backlash, fueled by media sensationalism and political maneuvers, forced psilocybin into the shadows. Today, we stand on the brink of a new era, a "psychedelic renaissance," where rigorous research and changing perceptions are reclaiming psilocybin's place as both a therapeutic marvel and a key to deeper self-understanding.

Chapter 2
Understanding Psilocybin

Imagine for a moment finding yourself in a green forest where the air is rich with the scent of earth and the soft hum of nature surrounds you. Suddenly, your eyes catch a cluster of enigmatic mushrooms casting a subtle yet enchanting glow under the shade of the trees, not just any ordinary mushrooms but the bearers of psilocybin, also known as the mysterious compound that has woven stories of spiritual awakening, artistic inspiration, and profound self-reflection for those who have ventured into its quest to find solace.

Psilocybin has been revered by Indigenous cultures around the world and viewed as a bridge between the earthly and the ethereal for centuries throughout history. But what is it about this compound that has captured the curiosity of mystics, artists, and now scientists of the modern world, and how does such a small molecule contained within a tiny mushroom lead to profound transformations in human consciousness and health?

Let's explore psilocybin on a molecular level and dive into the very core of psilocybin. Along the way, we will decode the cryptic language of organic chemistry and see how psilocybin stands shoulder-to-shoulder with intriguing relatives like psilocin, DMT, and even the mood-regulating serotonin and other chemicals that naturally exist in our brains.

Let us also journey through the body, navigating the complex maze of metabolism where psilocybin undergoes its magical transformation. We'll explore the brain, that intricate maestro of our body that directs the orchestra of our thoughts, emotions, and senses. It is a hub of the neural symphony, home to the harmonious interplay of neurotransmitters, receptors, and signals that culminates in the vivid tapestries of a psilocybin voyage.

Understanding Psilocybin

Psilocybin, often known as the "magic molecule," has gained significant attention in recent years for its potentially therapeutic and healing effects. While ancient civilizations have long revered the mystical properties of this compound, modern science has only just begun to unravel its true potential. All these potential benefits stem from its unique molecular structure.

The Molecular Structure of Psilocybin

Before our deep exploration of psilocybin, let us take a moment to establish some fundamental concepts of organic chemistry. Organic chemistry, often seen as the "chemistry of life," investigates the compounds primarily composed of carbon and hydrogen, which may include nitrogen, oxygen, sulfur, phosphorus, and a few other elements. It's a vast and complex field of science that offers a framework to understand the structure, composition, and behavior of molecules like psilocybin.

Basic Principles of Organic Chemistry

• Atoms and Bonds

Organic chemistry is all about the atoms and the bonds they form with each other. As you might remember from chemistry class, the most common types of bonds are covalent (sharing electron pairs between atoms) and ionic (transferring electrons from one atom to another).

• Functional Groups

Functional groups are specific clusters of atoms within molecules that determine characteristic reactions of those molecules. They play a significant role in defining the properties and reactivity of organic compounds.

• Isomers

Isomers are those compounds with identical molecular formulas but distinct molecular structures and arrangements. They exemplify the diversity of organic chemistry.

Psilocybin and Other Molecules

Now that we have a basic understanding of organic chemistry, let us decipher the molecule of psilocybin.

Psilocybin is an indole-based compound that comprises a six-membered benzene ring fused to a five-membered nitrogen-containing pyrrole ring (Mitra et al., 2021). This structure forms the core of many organic compounds, including those with physiological activity in animals.

In a psilocybin molecule, the indole ring is attached to a phosphoric acid group. This phosphorylated structure is one of the reasons why psilocybin is inactive when ingested. It becomes active after dephosphorylation into psilocin by the body.

The molecule's exact chemical name is 4-phosphoryl oxy-N. N-dimethyltryptamine, which might seem a mouthful, but offers an insight into its structure. The "4-phosphoryl oxy" stipulates the position of the phosphoric acid group on the indole ring. At the same time "N, N-dimethyl" tells us about the two methyl groups attached to the nitrogen atom of the tryptamine structure.

As we discussed above, when psilocybin is ingested, it gets converted into psilocin. This resembles psilocybin in structure but lacks the phosphoric acid group. This makes psilocin active and responsible for the psychedelic effects. Its chemical name, 4-HO-DMT (4-hydroxy-dimethyltryptamine), points to the hydroxyl (-OH) group that replaces the phosphate group in psilocybin.

DMT (Dimethyltryptamine)

DMT, like psilocybin and psilocin, belongs to the tryptamine class. It lacks the hydroxyl or phosphate group in psilocin and psilocybin, respectively. This mystic chemical is a powerful hallucinogenic compound found in various plants and animals.

Chris J. Conlan

Serotonin

Serotonin is perhaps the most significant molecule to compare with psilocybin as they are relatives. It is a neuro-transmitter and plays a critical role in mood regulation. Its structure is strikingly similar to that of psilocybin and psilocin. Serotonin also has an indole ring, but instead of the additional groups seen in psilocybin and psilocin, it has a hydroxyl group and an amine group in specific locations. The close structural resemblance between serotonin and psilocin is the primary reason psilocin interacts with serotonin recep-tors in the brain.

The compounds in "magic mushrooms" have danced through history, religion, and science, consistently proving their significance and making important breakthroughs in these fields.

The Metabolism of Psilocybin

When you hear the word "psilocybin," images of colorful mushrooms with potent mind-altering and healing properties might dance before your eyes. These mushrooms, commonly known as "magic mushrooms," contain psilocybin, which has been central to spiritual rituals, academic studies, and recre-ational adventures for centuries. But have you ever wondered how a small bite of a mushroom can lead to vibrant visions and profound introspection and hallucinations? To understand this, let us explore the metabolic processes of the human body.

The Role of the Body in Processing Substances

Before exploring psilocybin's unique metabolic journey, it's important to understand how our bodies process different substances to establish the basic knowledge base for appreciating the magic behind the "magic mushroom."

Every substance we consume, from the food we eat and the water we drink to the medications or recreational drugs we might take, is processed by our body to either harness its benefits or eliminate potential toxins. The liver beneath the diaphragm is our body's primary detoxification center. Known as the body's chemical processing plant, our liver plays a pivotal role in breaking down and converting different substances so they can either be used by the body or expelled.

The liver achieves this through a series of chemical reactions. These reactions usually involve enzymes—specialized proteins that speed up the breakdown or conversion of substances. The two-phase system, Phase I and Phase II detoxification, is typically how the liver deals with most substances. Phase I often converts a toxin into a less harmful form or even into a more reactive form that can then be further processed in Phase II. On the other hand, in Phase II, these products are made water-soluble which allows them to be eliminated from the body through urine or feces.

From Psilocybin to Psilocin

Now that we have the backdrop of general metabolism in our mind, let's hone in on the specifics of psilocybin. When we consume a magic mushroom, we are not directly ingesting the compound which is responsible for the psychedelic experience. Instead, we are ingesting the precursor known as the psilocybin.

Once inside the body, the liver takes center stage. An enzyme called alkaline phosphatase present in the liver facilitates the conversion of psilocybin into psilocin. In this process, a phosphate group is removed from psilocybin, turning it into an active form called psilocin.

But you may ask, why does the body not directly react to psilocybin? The answer to this question lies in the molecular structure of psilocybin and our brain's receptors. Psilocin is more adept at crossing the blood-brain barrier, a protective barrier that regulates which substances can influence brain function. Once psilocin successfully permeates this barrier, it can interact with certain receptors in the brain known as the serotonin receptors. This interaction induces major psychedelic experiences, such as visual hallucinations, deep emotional introspection, and a distorted sense of time and space.

The Implications

The metabolic transformation of psilocybin into psilocin is not free from implications. This process has several impacts:

Onset of Effects

The time it takes for psilocybin to be converted to psilocin and produce psychedelic effects can vary from person to person. This duration depends on individual factors like metabolism rate, liver function, and what you have eaten at the time of ingestion. Hence, some users might experience a faster onset of effects than others.

Duration and Intensity

As the body continues to process and break down psilocin, the intensity of the psychedelic experience may wane with time. The effects of psilocin, being an active compound, fade away and is metabolized further and excreted. This is why, after a certain period (that varies from person to person), the effects of the mushroom diminish, and the user "comes down" from their trip to the heavens.

Toxicity

The liver's ability to efficiently convert psilocybin to psilocin and then break down psilocin plays a critical role in the compound's safety profile. While magic mushrooms are generally considered to have low toxicity, overconsumption can still lead to potential liver stress. This is why it is very important to treat the compound with extreme caution and respect.

Variability of Experience

Given that every person has a different metabolic rate and liver efficiency, the experience of two people consuming the same amount of psilocybin can be markedly different. Genetics, overall health, liver function, and concurrent use of other substances can influence how quickly psilocybin is converted to psilocin and how it is experienced by the person consuming it.

Interactions With Other Chemicals

The liver metabolizes many other substances we consume. Therefore, using psilocybin, along with other substances and medications, can influence its processing, ultimately altering the duration, intensity, or safety of the trip.

In conclusion, the psychedelic journey induced by magic mushrooms is not just a mere play of sensory perceptions but is deeply rooted in the intricate biochemistry of our bodies. With its transformative abilities, the liver serves as the unsung hero in this narrative, orchestrating the conversion of psilocybin to its active, mind-altering form, psilocin. As with all substances, understanding the science behind the experience equips us with the knowledge to approach its use with respect, caution, and wonder.

How Psilocybin Interacts With the Human Brain?

Our brain, often considered to be the body's most intricate and enigmatic organ, stands at the nexus of our thoughts, emotions, actions, and memories. Weighing approximately three pounds, this mysterious organ is composed of billions of neurons responsible for transmitting signals to the rest of our body. Our brain has the following main parts:

The Cerebrum

It is the largest part of our brain, responsible for thinking, perceiving, producing, and understanding language. It is further divided into four lobes (Cherry, 2020):

- The Frontal Lobe is responsible for reasoning, problem-solving, and voluntary movement (*Frontal Lobe: What It Is, Function, Location & Damage*, 2022).
- The Parietal Lobe handles sensory information and spatial orientation.
- The Temporal Lobe is concerned with memory, hearing, and emotion.
- The Occipital Lobe primarily deals with vision.

The Cerebellum

It is located under the cerebrum and plays a critical role in movement coordination and maintaining posture and balance of the body.

The Brainstem

It connects the cerebrum and cerebellum to the spinal cord and facilitates many vital automotive functions, such as breathing, regulating heart rate, and regulating body temperature (*Brainstem: Overview, Function & Anatomy*. Cleveland Clinic).

The Limbic System

Our Limbic system comprises several interconnected structures deep within the brain. It governs emotions, memories, and certain habits. Major structures include the amygdala, which is responsible for emotional reactions, and the hippocampus, which is central to memory formation.

The Neurotransmitter System

Neurotransmitters are endogenous chemicals that bridge the communication gap between our brain's neurons. They function by transmitting signals from a neuron to a target cell, which can be another neuron, muscle cell, or gland cell. One of the most discussed and significant neurotransmitters is serotonin.

Serotonin is commonly known as the "feel-good neurotransmitter" because it has profound implications on mood, emotion, sleep, and appetite. Roughly 90% of our body's serotonin is found in the gastrointestinal tract, but the remainder, which affects mood and cognition, is produced in our brain (Terry & Margolis, 2017).

The synthesis of serotonin starts with the amino acid tryptophan, which transforms into 5-hydroxytryptophan (5-HTP) with the help of tryptophan hydroxylase. This 5-HTP then becomes serotonin, also known as 5-hydroxytryptamine (5-HT) in biochemistry language.

After its synthesis, the serotonin is stored in vesicles and is released into the synaptic gap when prompted. From here, it is able to bind to and activate receptors of the receiving neuron, leading to multiple cellular responses. Once its job is done, serotonin is taken back up into the releasing neuron, where it can be repackaged into vesicles or broken down by monoamine oxidase.

How Psilocin Interacts With Serotonin Receptors

Psilocybin found in magic mushrooms has been the focal point of multiple research studies due to its profound effects on human cognition and emotion. When psilocybin is ingested, it is swiftly converted into psilocin, the compound that interacts directly with the brain.

Psilocin is structurally related to serotonin; thus, it can mimic its effects in the brain. Psilocin acts primarily by binding to serotonin receptors, particularly the 5-HT2A receptor. When psilocin binds to this receptor, it induces a cascade of events that alter normal serotonin signaling.

A fascinating facet of psilocin's interaction with 5-HT2A receptors is its biased (functionally selective) agonism. This means that while serotonin and psilocin might both activate the same receptor, they can cause different downstream effects. Psilocin tilts the balance, favoring the psychedelic signaling pathway over the default serotonin one. This biased signaling likely plays a mind-altering role in producing the unique cognitive and perceptual effects of psychedelics.

Psilocin's interaction with the 5-HT2A receptor also leads to the increased release of glutamate, another neurotransmitter in our brain. This surge in glutamate contributes to the altered states of consciousness experienced during a psychedelic trip.

Similarly, emerging research studies hint at psychedelics, like psilocin, inducing changes in brain plasticity. Psilocin might amplify the expression of factors like glutamate and brain-derived neurotrophic factor (BDNF). The latter plays a critical role in neuronal growth and the health of our brain and its association with mood disorders, like depression, could illuminate potential therapeutic avenues for psilocybin (Ly et al., 2018).

The hallucinations we experience after consuming the magic mushrooms are because the 5-HT2A receptors are densely located in the visual cortex. This density probably accounts for the visual hallucinations and distortions characteristic of psilocybin experiences. When these receptors are blocked, the visual effects of psilocybin are often diminished, further cementing the relationship between the two.

In a nutshell, the dynamics between psilocybin and the brain is an intricate complex interplay of perception and neural signaling. As research in the field of psilocybin continues, we edge closer to a more holistic understanding of not just psilocybin, but the very fabric of our consciousness and the chemistry of our brain chemicals. Whether for therapeutic application or pure scientific curiosity, the journey into the heart of the human mind is bound to be an enlightening one that needs further exploration.

The Side Effects of Psilocybin

Psilocybin, the principal psychoactive component of "magic mushrooms," has intrigued both recreational users and scientific researchers for decades. Its profound impact on sensory perception, cognition, and emotion presents a unique profile of effects and side effects that deserves thorough exploration.

Visual Alterations

Psilocybin can greatly intensify and transform visual perceptions. Users often report vivid colors, geometric patterns, and a world that seems alive. This isn't just about seeing imaginary things. Inanimate objects may appear to breathe or move, walls might undulate, and textures can take on a pronounced three-dimensionality. These visual effects can be profoundly beautiful or disconcerting, depending on the individual's mindset and environment.

Auditory Sensations

Beyond the visual domain, psilocybin can heighten hearing. Some describe echoes or auditory hallucinations, such as hearing music or sounds that aren't present. These alterations can add to the richness of the experience or become overwhelming in certain situations.

Altered Perception of Time

A common report among psilocybin users is the distortion of time. Minutes can feel like hours. This temporal dislocation can be either liberating, providing a sense of timelessness, or anxiety-inducing, if one becomes fixated on its passage.

Derealization and Depersonalization

The very fabric of reality can feel altered under psilocybin. Users might feel that the world around them isn't real or that they're watching themselves from a distance. This dream-like detachment can be both enlightening and unsettling.

Tactile Sensations

The world doesn't just look and sound different; it can feel different too. Users often describe unique physical sensations, such as a sense of interconnectedness with their surroundings or the blurring of boundaries between themselves and the world around them.

Euphoria

Many users seek psilocybin for its capacity to induce feelings of profound well-being and happiness. This intense joy can feel transcendent and all-encompassing.

Spiritual Awakening

For some, the psilocybin experience feels deeply spiritual. They report feelings of interconnectedness, encounters with divine entities, or insights into the nature of existence.

Distorted Thinking

Linear thinking can be challenging. Thoughts might spiral, bifurcate, or come in rapid or fragmented bursts. For some, this can be creatively inspiring, while for others, it can be disorienting.

Nausea and Vomiting

Especially common when consuming raw mushrooms, gastrointestinal distress can be a side effect. For many, this initial discomfort gives way to the psychedelic experience, but it can be off-putting for some.

Dilated Pupils

This physiological response can lead to a heightened sensitivity to light and altered visual perceptions.

Drowsiness

Fatigue, yawning, and a sense of lethargy are common, especially as the effects of the psilocybin start to wear off.

Hallucinogen Persisting Perception Disorder (HPPD)

Some users report flashbacks to hallucinations, even weeks or months after taking the drug. This re-experiencing can be disconcerting and, in some cases, distressing.

Psychosis

In rare cases, individuals might exhibit behaviors or thought patterns similar to the symptoms of schizophrenia. This can include paranoia, delusions, or disorganized thinking.

Bad Trips

Arguably one of the most feared side effects, a "bad trip" can encompass terrifying hallucinations, profound paranoia, and intense anxiety. The experience can be traumatic and can lead to subsequent psychological distress.

Ensuring a Safe Experience

Ensuring a safe and healthy experience is one of the most crucial factors in determining the nature of a psilocybin experience. Being in a calm, familiar, and secure environment, preferably with a sober and experienced trip-sitter, can greatly influence the direction of the trip.

- Start with a low dose to gauge the body's reaction. It's always easier to take more later than to deal with an overpoweringly intense experience.
- Keeping the body hydrated and having some light, easy-to-digest foods available can help counteract some of the physical side effects.
- Combining psilocybin with alcohol, cannabis, or other drugs can create unpredictable, and sometimes dangerous, effects.
- If things get challenging, grounding oneself with the knowledge that the effects are temporary can be reassuring.
- If someone seems in distress, physically or psychologically, it's essential to seek professional help.
- With its varied legal status worldwide, being aware of local regulations is crucial.
- Taking time afterward to rest, reflect, and process the experience is essential. This can involve journaling, discussing the experience with others, or seeking guidance from a therapist or support group familiar with psychedelic experiences.

While psilocybin presents a vast spectrum of experiences, from the enlightening to the challenging, being informed and cautious is paramount. Knowledge, respect for the substance, and prioritizing safety can ensure the most beneficial and least harmful encounters with this ancient and potent compound.

Overview of Long-Term Effects

The intrigue surrounding the effects of psilocybin, a naturally occurring compound found in certain mushroom species, has grown over the past few decades. Historically rooted in spiritual and ceremonial practices, its modern resurgence in scientific research and recreational use has led to a greater understanding of its psychological impacts. Let us explore the long-term effects, both beneficial and adverse, stemming from psilocybin use.

Potential Lasting Effects

Research has noted that psilocybin can lead to profound experiences that might impact an individual's personality, especially in the domains of openness and creativity. Participants often describe feelings of interconnectedness with nature, the universe, or a higher power, sometimes leading to increased environmental awareness and altruistic behavior.

Emotional Well-Being

A study spearheaded by Mans, Kettner, Erritzoe, and their colleagues in 2021 delved into the lasting impacts of psychedelics on mental well-being. Their results showed sustained improvements in well-being up to two years after psychedelic experiences. This enhancement was seen in two main factors:

Staying Well

This leans more toward a future-facing outlook, indicating attributes like resilience, psychological flexibility, and mindfulness. Such characteristics not only ensure personal growth but also serve as protective factors against mental stressors.

This evidence points to the possibility of psychedelics, including psilocybin, fostering a holistic increase in emotional health, both in the present moment and in preparation for future challenges.

Potential Risks

While the potential benefits of psilocybin are fascinating, the potential risks it bring cannot be overlooked:

Psychological Distress

A "bad trip" on psilocybin can be a harrowing experience characterized by intense fear, paranoia, and feelings of impending doom. These episodes can be so profound that they leave a lasting imprint, leading to subsequent anxiety or phobic reactions. For some, the very unpredictability of whether a trip will be "good" or "bad" is anxiety-provoking in itself.

Hallucinogen Persisting Perception Disorder (HPPD)

HPPD is a rare, but documented, side effect of hallucinogenic use. It involves recurring visual disturbances and hallucinations that emerge without warning, sometimes days, months, or even years after the initial drug experience. Such symptoms can be distressing, especially when mistaken for severe neurological conditions like a stroke or brain tumor.

Persistent Psychosis

Although rare, some individuals may experience persistent psychosis post-hallucinogen use. This includes ongoing mental disturbances like visual disruptions, paranoia, disorganized thinking, and mood swings. It's yet to be fully understood why certain individuals are more susceptible to these adverse outcomes.

Emerging Research on Therapeutic Applications of Psilocybin

Historically, the allure of psychedelic substances like LSD and psilocybin mushrooms, was mostly within the realms of counter-culture. Fast-forward to today, these compounds are at the heart of innovative scientific studies aiming to uncover their therapeutic potential.

Recent trials have primarily focused on psilocybin's potential therapeutic value. Preliminary results have been promising, showcasing the substance's potential to alleviate symptoms of depression, anxiety, PTSD, and addiction. Additionally, the Multidisciplinary Association for Psychedelic Studies (MAPS) has been instrumental in pushing the boundaries of this research.

LSD Research

Since its serendipitous discovery in 1938 by Albert Hofmann, LSD's relationship with the therapeutic world has been a roller-coaster. The 1950s and 1960s saw a wave of research into its therapeutic applications, especially in treating anxiety, depression, psychosomatic diseases, and addiction. Although overshadowed by societal concerns and legal restrictions, contemporary interest in its therapeutic potential has reignited. A systematic review of controlled and randomized clinical trials has affirmed LSD's potential, notably in addressing alcoholism.

Depression & Anxiety

Psilocybin therapy, especially when combined with psychotherapy, has shown remarkable potential in alleviating depressive symptoms. Similarly, LSD, during its heyday in the 1950s and 1960s, was employed to trigger behavioral and personality changes, targeting conditions like depression and anxiety.

Addiction

One of the more pronounced areas of success for LSD therapy, as indicated by the aforementioned systematic review, was in treating alcoholism. This could herald a new era of addiction treatment, steering away from traditionally-employed opioids.

End-of-Life Psychological Distress

Psychedelics, due to their potential to catalyze profound spiritual or existential experiences, may assist individuals in coming to terms with their mortality. Studies from the mid-20th century showed that LSD, coupled with appropriate guidance, could help reduce pain, anxiety, and depression in terminally ill patients.

Safety Concerns

Classic hallucinogens, like LSD, can sometimes lead to "bad trips" or "challenging experiences," typified by anxiety, dysphoria, and confusion. These experiences, especially in unsupervised settings, can result in unpredictable behaviors. A more severe concern is the potential exacerbation of psychotic disorders. Proper screening for prior psychotic episodes and predispositions is essential.

Cardiovascular Concerns

Hallucinogens, while exhibiting low physiological toxicity, can lead to modest increases in blood pressure and heart rate. Hence, they might not be suitable for those with severe cardiovascular diseases.

Societal Stigma & Legal Restrictions

The societal perceptions and legal limitations surrounding psychedelics, especially LSD, can't be ignored. Historically, these substances have been associated with counter-culture movements, leading to their classification among the most restricted psychoactive substances. These restrictions have curtailed research and potentially beneficial therapeutic applications.

Designing Appropriate Clinical Trials

The very nature of psychedelics makes them challenging to study. The effects they produce are often subjective and deeply personal. Designing double-blind clinical trials that stand up to contemporary scientific scrutiny is challenging but essential for a deeper understanding.

The renaissance of research into psychedelics, primarily LSD and psilocybin, is a testament to the ever-evolving nature of therapeutic science. As more studies shed light on their potential benefits and methods to mitigate their risks, society might find itself on the cusp of a paradigm shift in treating an array of psychological conditions. Yet, as with all pioneering ventures, the journey requires caution, patience, and a commitment to scientific rigor.

Conclusion

Chapter 2 offered a comprehensive exploration of psilocybin, from its intricate molecular structure to its profound impacts on the human psyche. We explored the molecular nuances, comparing psilocybin to its closely related molecules, and we looked at the similarities with other compounds. The body's metabolic transformation of psilocybin to psilocin was highlighted, a pivotal process that sets the stage for the compound's psychedelic effects. This conversion plays a crucial role when psilocin, the active form, interfaces with the brain's neurotransmitter system, particularly the serotonin receptors, manifesting the array of acute sensory and cognitive experiences users report. While the immediate effects can range from sensory distortions to profound cognitive shifts, acknowledging the spectrum of side effects, both short-lived and persistent is important. The long-term implications of psilocybin usage, whether beneficial shifts in personality and emotional well-being or risks like HPPD, indicate the substance's dual nature. Recent therapeutic research paints a promising picture, with psilocybin showing potential in treating various psychological ailments. Yet, as with all emerging therapies, the call for further research and a balanced understanding of its benefits and risks remains paramount.

Chapter 3
Why Grow Your Own?

In the soft glow of the morning light, Eleanor tenderly inspects her latest batch of home-grown mushrooms. The delicate, fleshy caps have just started to unfold, revealing their true form and potential. As she holds one between her fingers, feeling the connection with this organism she nurtured from a mere spore, a sense of pride swells within her. She's not just a casual observer of the natural world; she's an active participant in it.

Welcome to the chapter where we explore the intriguing world of growing your own psilocybin mushrooms—a task that proves to be more than just a simple hobby for many; it's a transformative experience.

Imagine how empowering it would be to control the strain and potency of your own cultivation, tailoring each batch to suit your own needs or curiosities, just like Eleanor. Think of the satisfaction that comes from knowing you've cultivated health as much as you've grown mushrooms, thanks to the meticulous avoidance of harmful contaminants. There's a certain peace of mind in knowing that the mushrooms you consume are pure and safe because you raised them yourself in a clean and controlled environment.

Growing your own mushrooms isn't just about the end product. It's about the journey. Eleanor doesn't just grow mushrooms; she grows her knowledge and understanding of the world. Each cultivation cycle is more than a growing process; it's a live, hands-on lesson in mycology and botany. Her backyard is her living, breathing classroom, offering a profound connection to the intricate lives of fungi and a deeper relationship with the science of this remarkable kingdom.

But it's not just about Eleanor, or you, or the mushrooms. It's bigger than that. It's about the world we live in. Choosing to cultivate your own mushrooms can be a thoughtful nod to sustainability—an alternative to wild harvesting that respects and preserves our natural ecosystems. It's about mindful consumption and considering how our choices, even in the sharing of homegrown psilocybin, reverberate through our communities. It's about engaging with the profound ethical questions that come with this newfound empowerment.

So, why grow your own? As Eleanor's experience beautifully illustrates, the reasons are rich and multifaceted. Whether for personal use, education, ethical considerations, or a deeper connection to nature—cultivating your own psilocybin mushrooms can be a deeply rewarding endeavor.

Let's grow together and explore the lush, complex, and enlightening world of home mushroom cultivation.

The Benefits of Home Cultivation of Mushrooms

In an age where self-sustainability and natural living are increasingly valued, the home cultivation of mushrooms stands out as an enriching and rewarding endeavor. Beyond the pleasure of watching a spore transform into a fully grown mushroom, cultivating mushrooms at home presents several unique and tangible benefits. In this extensive guide, we'll delve into the multifaceted advantages of growing mushrooms at home, highlighting the sense of accomplishment, control over strains and potency, and cost-effectiveness.

Home cultivation of mushrooms is much more than a practical endeavor; it is a profound act of engagement with the natural world. Each step, from inoculating a substrate with mycelium to harvesting the mature mushrooms, engenders a deep sense of connection with nature and the cycles of growth and decay that sustain life on Earth. Nurturing mushrooms from spores to fruiting bodies brings a sense of accomplishment that is hard to rival. It's akin to nurturing a part of the world, fostering growth, and being rewarded with tangible, edible results.

Mental Health Benefits

Recent studies have highlighted the therapeutic potential of "nature engagement"—activities like gardening and mushroom cultivation. Tending to a living organism, understanding its needs, and watching it grow can be meditative and may reduce stress, depression, and anxiety.

Strain Selection and Mastery

With home cultivation, you are in the driver's seat. Advanced techniques, like agar plate strain selection, allow for precise control over the mushroom strain you grow. This process involves inoculating petri dishes with spores, selecting the most vigorous mycelium, and using this to inoculate your substrate. By selecting specific strains, cultivators can also exert control over the potency of the mushrooms they grow, which is an important consideration for both medicinal and psychedelic varieties.

Quality Control

Growing at home means that you know exactly what goes into your cultivation process. This means you can avoid harmful pesticides and ensure the cleanest, highest-quality produce possible.

Cost-Effectiveness

While the initial setup for home mushroom cultivation—including purchasing a laminar flow hood, a pressure cooker, and other equipment—can be somewhat costly, these are largely one-time investments. Spawn bags, for instance, are a cost-effective way to produce large batches of substrate.

Growing in Bulk

Monotubs are praised for their high yields and simplicity. By adopting such methods, home cultivators can produce signifi-cant quantities of mushrooms at a fraction of the purchasing cost.

Infinite Potential

With techniques such as self-healing injection ports, the process becomes less prone to contamination, more efficient, and, thus, more cost-effective. Furthermore, by mastering agar techniques, you can maintain a continuous culture, essentially enabling an endless supply of mushrooms from an initial spore syringe.

In a world that is increasingly disconnected from nature, home cultivation of mushrooms offers a deeply enriching, educational, and practical counterpoint. It is an invitation to engage with the living world in a hands-on way, to foster growth, and to reap the rewards of patience and care.

Through meticulous strain selection and careful cultivation practices, growers can tailor their mushrooms to their specific desires and needs. Beyond the profound sense of accomplishment and connection this practice can bring, it is also a highly cost-effective endeavor, turning a modest initial investment into a potentially endless supply of fresh, high-quality mushrooms.

Avoiding Harmful Contaminants in Mushroom Cultivation

Mushroom cultivation can be a rewarding endeavor, but it comes with its challenges. One of the most critical aspects of mushroom cultivation is maintaining purity in the growing environment. This involves understanding potential contaminants, the importance of sterilization and cleanliness, and verifying the health and purity of the crop. In this extensive guide, we will delve into the nitty-gritty of these critical aspects of mushroom cultivation.

Potential Contaminants and Their Risks

Molds and Fungi

Molds like Trichothecium, Neurospora, and Rhizopus can pose significant threats. They compete with mushroom mycelium for nutrients, potentially inhibiting mushroom growth. Some, like Rhizopus, are fast-growing and can rapidly colonize a substrate, essentially hijacking it from the desired mushroom species.

Bacteria

Common bacterial contaminants like Bacillus and Pseudomonas can spoil a mushroom culture. Bacillus, for instance, causes a condition known as "Wet Spot," characterized by a slimy appearance and a strong unpleasant odor, rendering the substrate useless for mushroom cultivation.

Mycotoxins

Some molds produce toxic compounds known as mycotoxins. These toxins can contaminate the growing mushrooms and pose severe health risks to those who consume them.

Sterilization and Cleanliness

The fundamental step in the cultivation process is sterilization, which is the complete destruction of all forms of life on a substance or surface. Sterilization helps create an environment where mushroom mycelium can grow without competition from other organisms.

Quality and Yield

An unclean cultivation environment results in poor yields and lower-quality mushrooms. Consistent sterilization practices and cleanliness ensure that the mushrooms have the best chance for robust and healthy growth.

Health and Safety

Proper sterilization eliminates the risk of growing mushrooms that are contaminated with harmful pathogens or toxins, ensuring that the mushrooms are safe to consume.

Sterilization and Disinfection Methods

Substrates can be soaked in hot water or exposed to steam to kill contaminants. This is a common, eco-friendly, and effective method for small-scale cultivators.

Certain chemicals, like hydrogen peroxide or bleach solutions, can be used to sterilize substrates and equipment. These methods are effective but must be used with care due to the potential for chemical residues.

Pasteurization

Unlike sterilization, pasteurization doesn't aim to kill all microorganisms but rather to reduce the population of harmful pathogens to a level where they won't cause harm. This method allows some beneficial organisms to survive, which can help in defending against future contamination.

Ways to Verify Purity and Health of the Crop

Healthy mycelium generally appears as a bright white, fluffy mass. Any discoloration or unusual textures (like sliminess) may be signs of contamination.

Odor

Healthy mushroom mycelium has an earthy, fresh smell. Sour, unpleasant, or off odors can be signs of bacterial contamination.

Lab Testing

For commercial growers or those who want to be extra sure of their crop's purity, lab testing can identify specific contaminants at the microscopic level.

Mushroom cultivation, while fulfilling, requires an understanding of the complex microbial world. Achieving a pure and potent crop of mushrooms is not just about promoting the growth of the fungi you want but is equally about warding off the myriad of potential contaminants that you don't want. Sterilization and cleanliness are not mere steps in the process; they are the bedrock on which successful mushroom cultivation is built.

Educational Aspects of Mycology and Botany

Mycology and botany offer unique insights into the natural world and are integral components of biology education. While botany explores the world of plants and their interactions with the environment, mycology focuses on fungi, a kingdom with remarkable diversity and ecological significance. The cultivation of fungi, such as psilocybin mushrooms, provides an excellent opportunity for hands-on learning in mycology, fostering a deeper understanding of fungal biology and its connections to botany.

Scientific Inquiry and Hypothesis Testing

Cultivation teaches students how to design experiments, manipulate variables, and test hypotheses. They can explore factors that influence fungal growth, such as temperature, humidity, and substrate composition, and gain an understanding of how environmental conditions shape the distribution and abundance of fungal species.

Genetics and Reproduction

Fungal cultivation allows students to study genetic variation and reproductive strategies in fungi. They can observe how fungi produce spores, either sexually or asexually, and track genetic markers across generations. Understanding the various methods of fungal reproduction, including plasmogamy, karyogamy, and meiosis, offers insights into the genetic diversity and adaptability of fungi.

Ecology and Symbiosis

By cultivating fungi, students learn about the ecological roles of fungi and their interactions with plants and other organisms. They can explore mutualistic relationships, such as mycorrhizal associations, where fungi exchange nutrients with plant roots, and discover how these partnerships influence plant health and ecosystem stability.

Physiology and Adaptation

Fungal cultivation sheds light on the physiological adaptations of fungi to different environmental conditions. Students can study how fungi respond to changes in temperature, moisture, and nutrient availability, and they can examine the strategies fungi use to survive and thrive in diverse habitats.

Biotechnology and Sustainable Agriculture

Mycology education offers opportunities to explore the applications of fungi in biotechnology and sustainable agriculture. Students can learn about the use of fungi in bioremediation, biofuel production, and sustainable farming practices. They can experiment with cultivating edible mushrooms and investigate the potential benefits of integrating fungi into agroecological systems.

Scientific Principles Through Cultivation

The cultivation of psilocybin mushrooms involves several scientific principles that enable a deeper understanding of fungal life cycles and ecology. Fungi reproduce sexually and asexually, and their life cycle consists of a series of growth and reproductive phases. When cultivating fungi, their life cycle starts with spores or mycelium, which germinate and grow, eventually producing mushrooms and releasing spores for the next generation.

Plasmogamy

Plasmogamy is a crucial step in the sexual reproduction of fungi, leading to the formation of a dikaryotic cell, which ultimately gives rise to new fungal offspring. This process involves the fusion of the cytoplasm of two compatible cells, usually from different individuals, resulting in a single cell containing two haploid nuclei (*Fungus—Reproductive Processes of Fungi*, 2019). In fungi, the nuclei typically remain separate and do not immediately fuse (karyogamy). Instead, they coexist within the same cell and divide synchronously, giving rise to a unique fungal stage called the dikaryon. The dikaryotic phase persists for a variable duration, depending on the fungal species, and eventually leads to karyogamy, where the two nuclei fuse to form a diploid nucleus. Subsequent meiosis produces haploid spores, which can germinate and grow into new individuals.

The occurrence of plasmogamy varies across fungal species and is influenced by factors such as mating type, pheromones, and environmental conditions. Plasmogamy occurs through multiple methods, as outlined below:

Planogametic Copulation

In this method, motile gametes (planogametes) of different individuals fuse, resulting in plasmogamy. This primitive mode of reproduction is observed in some lower fungi, where both gametes may be motile, or one gamete is motile while the other is non-motile.

Gametangial Contact

This process involves direct contact between two gametangia (specialized reproductive structures) of opposite mating types. The male nuclei migrate into the female gametangium, facilitating plasmogamy.

Gametangial Copulation

In this method, two gametangia come in contact and fuse, allowing their entire contents to mix. This can occur by the passage of contents from one gametangium to another through a pore or by the dissolution of the contacting walls, resulting in a common cell where the protoplasts mix.

Spermatization

This process involves the transfer of small, uninucleate, spore-like male structures (spermatia) to female gametangia or receptive hyphae, where plasmogamy occurs.

Somatogamy

In this method, somatic cells, rather than specialized reproductive structures, take on sexual function. Plasmogamy occurs through the fusion of somatic cells.

Applications Beyond Psilocybin Mushrooms

The knowledge acquired from cultivating psilocybin mushrooms extends far beyond this specific group of fungi. Understanding fungal reproduction, life cycles, and ecology enhances our comprehension of broader ecological and biological principles. The cultivation process teaches patience, observation skills, and problem-solving, as cultivators must optimize conditions for healthy fungal growth and address any issues that arise.

Additionally, cultivating mushrooms can promote the appreciation of nature's intricate relationships, biodiversity, and the importance of protecting our environment. Cultivation can also foster curiosity and inspire individuals to further explore the fields of mycology and botany, leading to increased scientific literacy, research contributions, or even career opportunities in these disciplines.

Cultivating mushrooms, including psilocybin-containing fungi, provides an opportunity to delve deep into the world of mycology and botany. The scientific principles learned through cultivation offer valuable insights into fungal life cycles and ecology, which extend beyond psilocybin mushrooms, and enrich our understanding of the natural world. Cultivating mushrooms can inspire individuals to explore these fields further, fostering a deeper appreciation for the interconnectedness of life and the importance of protecting our environment.

The Ethics and Environmental Impact of Home Cultivation

As we delve into the world of psychedelics, particularly the cultivation and use of psilocybin mushrooms, it is vital to consider the ethical and environmental implications of this practice. Psilocybin has a long history of use for spiritual, therapeutic, and recreational purposes, and with the recent resurgence of scientific research and decriminalization efforts, home cultivation is becoming increasingly common. We will examine the sustainability of home cultivation versus wild harvesting, discuss responsible use and sharing within communities, and explore the ethical implications of psilocybin cultivation and use.

Home Cultivation vs. Wild Harvesting

The issue of sustainability is central to the conversation surrounding home cultivation and the wild harvesting of psilocybin mushrooms. Each approach has its advantages and drawbacks.

Home Cultivation

Home cultivation allows for controlled growth, with precise knowledge of substrates and environmental conditions, ensuring the safety and potency of the mushrooms. This controlled environment also enables cultivators to optimize their yields and reduce the risk of contamination or the accidental consumption of toxic species.

From an environmental perspective, home cultivation can reduce the pressure on wild mushroom populations and the ecosystems they inhabit. However, there are trade-offs. Home cultivation requires resources such as substrates, containers, and energy for climate control. As a result, it may have a larger carbon footprint compared to wild harvesting, depending on the scale of cultivation and resource use efficiency.

Wild Harvesting

Wild harvesting, on the other hand, relies on the natural growth of mushrooms in their native environments. When done responsibly and sustainably, wild harvesting can have minimal environmental impact. However, overharvesting can deplete local populations and disrupt ecosystems. Wild mushrooms also play a vital role in nutrient cycling and soil health, and their removal can have cascading effects on the environment.

Moreover, wild harvesting carries the risk of misidentification. Some toxic mushroom species closely resemble psilocybin-containing varieties, and accidental ingestion can have severe health consequences.

Responsible Use and Sharing

With the increasing popularity of psilocybin mushrooms and the growing body of research supporting their therapeutic potential, it is essential to address the responsible use and sharing of these substances within communities.

Responsible use of psilocybin mushrooms entails understanding the effects, risks, and proper dosage, as well as considering one's mental and physical health, setting, and intentions. The "set and setting" concept emphasizes the importance of the user's mindset and the environment in shaping the psychedelic experience.

Psilocybin use can have profound and transformative effects, but it is not without risks. Individuals with a personal or family history of psychosis or certain mental health conditions may be at higher risk for adverse reactions. Moreover, mixing psilocybin with other substances, including prescription medications, can be dangerous.

Sharing and Community Impact

Sharing psilocybin mushrooms within communities raises ethical questions around informed consent, safety, and the potential for misuse. When sharing, it is essential to ensure that recipients understand the effects, risks, and proper usage and are in a suitable mental and physical state for the experience.

While psilocybin has the potential to foster community bonding, personal growth, and healing, its misuse can have negative consequences. Encouraging responsible use and providing harm reduction information is crucial to ensuring positive outcomes.

Ethical Implications

The cultivation and use of psilocybin mushrooms bring about several ethical considerations.

Cultural Respect

Psilocybin has a rich history of use in various cultures for spiritual and therapeutic purposes. As interest in psilocybin grows, it is essential to respect and acknowledge the traditions, knowledge, and practices of the Indigenous communities that have used these substances for generations.

Access and Equity

As psilocybin becomes more accepted and integrated into mainstream culture, there is a risk of commercialization and commodification, potentially leading to unequal access. It is essential to prioritize equitable access to psilocybin and its benefits, ensuring that marginalized and underserved communities are not left behind.

Consent and Autonomy

The use of psilocybin should be based on informed consent and personal autonomy. Individuals should have the right to access information, make informed decisions, and explore their consciousness without fear of legal repercussions.

Research and Regulation

As the scientific community continues to explore the thera-peutic potential of psilocybin, it is crucial to prioritize rigorous research and ethical considerations in the develop-ment of regulations and treatment protocols. Ensuring the safety, efficacy, and accessibility of psilocybin-assisted therapy is key to maximizing its benefits.

The cultivation and use of psilocybin mushrooms are complex topics with numerous ethical and environmental implications. Balancing sustainability, responsible use, cultural respect, and equitable access is essential to ensuring the positive impact of psilocybin on individuals and commu-nities alike. As we navigate this evolving landscape, it is vital to prioritize education, harm reduction, and ethical considera-tions every step of the way.

Conclusion

Chapter 3 explored the myriad reasons for growing your own psilocybin mushrooms, delving into the benefits of home cultivation and the importance of understanding purity and avoiding harmful contaminants. We discussed how home cultivation fosters a sense of accomplishment, connection to the natural world, control over strain and potency, and cost-effectiveness. Moreover, we examined the crucial role of sterilization and cleanliness in ensuring a pure and healthy crop, free from harmful contaminants like bacteria and molds. We also explored the educational aspects of mycology and botany, highlighting how cultivating mushrooms can lead to a deeper understanding of fungal life cycles and ecology, with applications extending beyond the world of psilocybin mushrooms. Lastly, we discussed the ethics and environmental impact of home cultivation, emphasizing the importance of balancing sustainability, responsible use, cultural respect, and equitable access. In essence, growing your own psilocybin mushrooms offers a holistic and enriching experience that extends beyond the psychedelic experience itself, fostering personal growth, knowledge, and ethical considerations that can be applied to various aspects of life.

Chapter 4
Identifying Psilocybin Mushrooms

In the dappled light of a dense, old-growth forest, where earthy scents and vibrant hues intertwine, a forager moves with care. To the casual observer, she might seem part of the natural rhythm of the woods. Her eyes scan the rich soil and decaying logs with the precision of an expert, seeking one of nature's most mystical and elusive treasures: psilocybin mushrooms. These fungi, with their uncanny ability to unlock profound mental and emotional landscapes, have fascinated people around the globe for centuries. But as our forager knows all too well, these miraculous mushrooms have doppelgangers—deceptive look-alikes, some of which harbor deadly poisons. For her, knowledge is not just power; it's survival.

Identifying psilocybin mushrooms is a delicate art steeped in science. It's a practice that demands a sharp eye, a discerning mind, and a healthy respect for the potential dangers lurking in misidentification. For the untrained eye, the colorful world of mushrooms can seem overwhelmingly complex, but with dedicated study, the intricate tapestry begins to unravel, revealing clear and identifiable threads.

This chapter will guide you through the intricate maze of mushroom taxonomy, shedding light on the families and genera where psilocybin species are found. We'll delve into the world of these incredible fungi, examining their defining characteristics—the subtle nuances and bold features alike that set them apart from their non-psychedelic counterparts. From the rolling pastures of North America to the rain-soaked woodlands of Europe, we'll journey across continents, exploring the diverse habitats where these mystical mushrooms choose to thrive.

As we navigate this vibrant world, we will introduce you to several of the most common and significant species within the psilocybin family. From the well-known Psilocybe cubensis, cherished by cultivators and foragers alike, to the potent Psilocybe azurescens of the Pacific Northwest, we will explore the unique identifying features, natural habitats, and the various effects they impart on the human mind.

But the path through this enthralling world is fraught with peril. For every safe and psychedelic species, there exists a sinister counterpart—a dangerous look-alike that could lead the uninformed forager toward severe poisoning or worse. We will draw sharp contrasts between these toxic twins and their psychedelic brethren, emphasizing the absolute necessity for certainty before one considers consumption.

To equip you with the tools necessary for safe and confident identification, we will guide you, step by step, in the art of making and interpreting spore prints—a vital practice for any aspiring mycologist. It's a process akin to developing a photograph, where the intricate details emerge slowly before your eyes, revealing the unique signature that each mushroom species leaves behind.

In the pages that follow, we walk a path between science and reverence, between curiosity and caution. With each step, we hope to arm you with the knowledge and respect required to safely unlock the profound and transformative potentials that psilocybin mushrooms offer. It's a path that a forager treads with grace and wisdom, and it's one that I invite you to join. Welcome to the world of psilocybin mushrooms.

Families and Genera of Psilocybin Mushrooms

Psilocybin mushrooms, colloquially known as "magic mushrooms," are a captivating group of fungi that have captured human interest for centuries due to their unique ability to produce psychedelic effects. Below, we will embark on an illuminating journey into the world of these remarkable fungi, tracing their taxonomy, identifying their key characteristics, and exploring their distribution and preferred habitats around the globe.

Overview of the Taxonomy of Fungi

Fungi are a diverse kingdom of organisms, distinct from plants, animals, and several other life forms. Within this kingdom, psilocybin mushrooms belong to the phylum Basidiomycota, which also includes the familiar mushrooms that might be found in a grocery store. The psilocybin-containing mushrooms primarily fall within two families: Psilocybe and Panaeolus, though a few other genera also contain species with these compounds.

Psilocybe Family

The genus Psilocybe is the most well-known of the psilocybin-containing mushrooms. Species within this genus are generally small to medium-sized and have a characteristic appearance, which includes a cap, stem, and gills beneath the cap where spores are produced.

Panaeolus Family

The Panaeolus genus is another significant group of psilocybin-containing mushrooms. These tend to have a more delicate, thin-stemmed appearance compared to Psilocybe species and often have a grey or mottled appearance.

Key Characteristics of Psilocybin Mushrooms

Psilocybin mushrooms are defined by their ability to produce psilocybin and psilocin, compounds that are responsible for their psychedelic effects. Here are some of the distinguishing features:

Chemical Composition

The defining feature of these mushrooms is their production of the alkaloids psilocybin and psilocin. These compounds interact with serotonin receptors in the human brain, leading to altered perception, mood, and consciousness.

Cap Appearance

Psilocybin mushrooms generally have a convex cap that may become flat or upturned with age. The surface can be smooth, silky, or slightly scaly, and the color can range from brown to golden, often changing as the mushroom matures or when it is bruised.

Bruising

A distinctive characteristic of many psilocybin-containing mushrooms is their tendency to bruise a blueish color when handled. This is due to the oxidation of psilocin, a phenomenon known as "bluing."

Spore Color

Typically, psilocybin mushrooms have a dark purple-brown to black spore print, which is a key identifying feature (Jay, 2020).

Habitat and Substrate

These mushrooms are often found growing on decaying plant material, such as wood and leaves, but some species grow in association with grasses or are dung-loving (coprophilous) (Alexander, 2023).

Global Distribution and Habitat Preferences

Psilocybin mushrooms are remarkably cosmopolitan, being found on multiple continents, often in regions with a temperate or tropical climate.

North America

From the forests of the Pacific Northwest to the southern reaches of Mexico, psilocybin mushrooms are found in a variety of habitats across North America.

Europe

Various species of psilocybin mushrooms are native to Europe, where they tend to prefer woodlands and grasslands.

Asia, Africa, and Oceania

In tropical regions, such as Southeast Asia and Central Africa, these mushrooms often grow in dense forests, while in Australia and New Zealand, they are commonly found in both wooded and open grassland areas.

Habitat Preferences

Psilocybin mushrooms are ecologically versatile. Some species prefer the decaying wood of forests, while others are found in rich, manured soils of grasslands or even along riverbanks and in marshy areas.

Climate Conditions

While some species prefer the consistent moisture and warmth of the tropics, others thrive in temperate climates, where they fruit during the wet, cooler months.

Psilocybin mushrooms are a fascinating and diverse group of fungi. Their unique chemical composition has not only spurred scientific and medical interest but has also entwined them deeply into the cultural fabric of various societies across the world. Understanding their taxonomy, key characteristics, and global distribution is essential for anyone looking to study or simply appreciate these remarkable organisms.

Detailed Profiles of Common Psilocybin Species

Psilocybe Cubensis

Psilocybe cubensis is one of the most recognizable and widely cultivated magic mushroom species. It is known for its golden-brown cap, which can be up to 8 cm in diameter, and its white stem. When bruised, the mushroom turns a bluish color due to the oxidation of psilocin. The gills are closely spaced and dark purple-brown with white or lilac edges.

Natural Habitats

This species thrives in subtropical environments and is commonly found in regions of South America, Central America, Southeast Asia, and Australia. In the wild, P. cubensis grows in dung or manure-rich soils, particularly those associated with cattle.

Growth Patterns

P. cubensis grows in dense clusters, usually during warm, rainy seasons. They thrive in high-humidity environments and require a nutritious substrate, like dung or grain-based concoctions, when cultivated at home.

Potency and Typical Effects

P. cubensis is known for its moderate to high potency. The effects of consuming this mushroom can include visual and auditory hallucinations, enhanced emotions, an altered perception of time, and profound introspective experiences. These effects can vary significantly depending on the dose and individual differences.

Psilocybe Semilanceata

Also known as the "liberty cap," Psilocybe semilanceata is characterized by its distinctive, sharply conical to bell-shaped cap. The cap is typically 5–25 mm in diameter. When wet, the cap becomes translucent and sticky. Its stem is slim, and the mushroom bruises blue when handled, similar to P. cubensis.

Natural Habitats

This species is common in the temperate regions of the Northern Hemisphere, particularly in Europe and North America. P. semilanceata prefers to grow in rich and acidic soil, often found in grassy fields, pastures, and meadows, particularly those that have been grazed by sheep or cows.

Growth Patterns

Liberty caps are generally solitary but can also be found in small groups. They flourish in the fall, especially after the first cold rain of the season.

Potency and Typical Effects

P. semilanceata is considered highly potent. It contains a high concentration of psilocybin and low amounts of psilocin. Users report intense visual experiences, deep emotional shifts, and a heightened sense of connection to nature.

Psilocybe Azurescens

Psilocybe azurescens, known as the "flying saucer mush-room," is one of the most potent psilocybin-containing species. It features a convex to flat, caramel or chestnut-brown cap when young, which fades to a lighter color with age. The cap is 30–100 mm in diameter. Like other Psilocybe species, it bruises blue when handled.

Natural Habitats

This species was initially discovered on the West Coast of the U.S., particularly in the area of the Columbia River Delta in Oregon and Washington. It grows vigorously in deciduous woodlands and prefers wood chips and sandy soils near dune grasses.

Growth Patterns

P. azurescens fruiting bodies typically appear in the fall and early winter. The mushrooms often grow in clusters and are found on decaying wood, especially in dune grasses or in landscaped areas where wood chips or mulch are used.

Potency and Typical Effects

Among the known Psilocybe species, P. azurescens stands out as one of the most potent. It is known for intense visual and auditory hallucinations, significant alterations in the perception of time and space, profound cognitive and philosophical insights, and deep emotional release.

The world of psilocybin-containing mushrooms is rich and varied. With distinct differences in appearance, habitat, growth patterns, and effects, each species presents a unique profile. Foragers and cultivators alike are encouraged to approach these mushrooms with respect and caution, and it is essential to have a deep understanding of each species for safe and informed use. As the field of psychedelic research continues to evolve, our understanding of these fascinating fungi, which have played a role in human history for thousands of years, continues to deepen and expand.

Dangerous Look-Alike Species

Mushrooms are fascinating organisms that grace our environment with an array of shapes, sizes, and colors. While some mushroom species are sought after for their medicinal properties or their culinary delights, others can be poisonous, even lethal. A critical concern arises when these poisonous species closely resemble their edible counterparts.

Amanita phalloides, commonly known as the Death Cap, is a perfect example of a dangerous mushroom. It bears a close resemblance to several edible mushrooms, including Amanita lanes (also known as "Fool's Mushroom") and some species of the Agaricus genus that are popular among foragers.

Galerina marginata, another toxic mushroom, can be easily mistaken for the psychoactive Psilocybe cubensis or the edible Armillaria mellea, also known as "Honey Fungus."

Key Differences

Let's take a closer look at the comparison between Galerina marginata and Psilocybe cubensis, two mushrooms that may look similar but have vastly different effects:

Cap Appearance

Galerina caps are often brown and can resemble the golden-brown cap of Psilocybe cubensis. However, Psilocybe caps are usually more distinctly golden and often exhibit a more pronounced "nipple" at the top.

Gill Color

Galerinas have brown gills, while Psilocybe cubensis's have gills that start out light grey and become dark purple-black as the mushroom matures.

Spore Print

Galerina spore prints are brown, whereas Psilocybe cubensis's spore prints are dark purple-black. Spore print color is a key feature in mushroom identification.

Bruising

Many Psilocybe species, including cubensis, bruise blue when handled due to the oxidation of psilocin. Galerinas do not exhibit this bluing reaction.

The Dangers of Misidentification

Misidentification of mushrooms can have severe consequences, including poisoning, organ failure, and death. For example, consuming a Death Cap (Amanita phalloides), even in small quantities, can result in severe liver and kidney damage. The insidious part is that symptoms may not appear until 6 to 24 hours after ingestion, at which point significant damage may have already occurred.

Given the high stakes, it's essential to underscore that no shortcut, folklore, or "quick test" can guarantee safe identification. The common myths, such as "safe if it can be peeled" or "safe if animals are eating it," are dangerously false. In fact, animals like squirrels can eat mushrooms that are deadly to humans without any ill effects.

The Importance of Identification Before Consumption

When it comes to foraging for wild mushrooms, the old adage, "When in doubt, throw it out," should be the guiding principle. Only absolute certainty, ideally confirmed by an expert mycologist, should suffice when deciding to consume a wild mushroom. Consulting field guides, taking spore prints, and examining mushrooms microscopically are steps toward safe identification, but even these can fall short without proper training and experience.

Consuming wild mushrooms without expert identification is akin to playing Russian roulette—with the stakes being severe illness or death. Even with edible mushrooms, improper preparation can lead to discomfort and illness, as some need to be cooked to neutralize compounds that can cause gastrointestinal distress.

For amateur foragers, sticking to well-known and easily identifiable species that have no poisonous look-alikes—such as Morels (Morchella spp.) or Chicken of the Woods (Laetiporus spp.)—is usually the safest route.

Why Are Mushrooms Poisonous?

While the specific role of toxins in some mushrooms remains unclear, they may serve various functions, including a defensive role in deterring consumption by animals or insects or a role in the mushroom's metabolism. For example, the peppery taste of some Russala and Lactarius species deters animals from eating them. In other cases, such as the deadly Amanita species, the toxins' role is not as apparent, as these mushrooms are reported to be good tasting, and their toxins have a delayed action that might not effectively deter consumption.

In a world where natural remedies and foraging are becoming increasingly popular, the risk of mushroom poisoning due to misidentification remains a severe and ever-present danger. The consequences of mistaking a toxic look-alike for a sought-after edible or psychoactive mushroom are grave and can be fatal. Thus, education, caution, and consultation with experts are paramount for anyone interested in mushroom foraging. The potential risks, including severe poisoning and death, far outweigh the benefits of consuming wild mushrooms without absolute certainty of their identity.

Making and Interpreting Spore Prints

Mushroom foraging is a delightful activity that allows us to connect with nature while discovering a variety of delicious and fascinating fungi. However, it's essential to identify mushrooms correctly, as some can be toxic or even lethal. That's where spore prints come in—a simple yet invaluable tool for accurate mushroom identification. In this guide, we will walk through the step-by-step process of making a spore print, discuss how to interpret them, and highlight the critical role they play for foragers.

Step-By-Step Guide to Making a Spore Print

Materials Needed

1. A mature mushroom
2. White and black paper or cardstock
3. A knife or scissors
4. A glass or jar
5. A clock or timer

Step 1: Harvest the Mushroom

Find a mature mushroom—ideally one with a cap that has fully opened, indicating that the gills are fully exposed and ready to release spores.

Step 2: Prepare the Mushroom

With a knife or scissors, cut off the stem of the mushroom close to the cap. This leaves you with just the cap, which contains the spore-producing gills or pores.

Step 3: Place the Cap on the Paper

Lay the cap, gills, or pores down on a piece of paper. Using both black and white paper can help since spore colors show up differently on contrasting backgrounds.

Step 4: Cover the Cap

Place a glass or jar over the mushroom cap to create a humid environment, encouraging the spores to release.

Step 5: Wait

Allow the cap to sit for several hours, typically between 4 and 24. This gives the mushroom ample time to release its spores onto the paper.

Step 6: Reveal and Preserve

After waiting, carefully lift the glass and the mushroom cap. You should see a spore print on the paper. To preserve the print, you can spray it lightly with hairspray for fixative.

Interpreting Spore Prints

Color

The color of a spore print can range from white, cream, and yellow to various shades of brown, black, and even vibrant colors like pink or purple. Each mushroom species produces a characteristic spore color, making this a vital clue in identification.

Pattern

While the color is usually uniform, the arrangement or pattern can vary. A clear and distinct print suggests a mature and healthy specimen, whereas a smudged or irregular pattern might indicate that the specimen was disturbed during printing.

Other Features

Sometimes, the thickness of the spore deposit, its edge characteristics, or other minute features can provide additional information, but these are generally of more interest to advanced mycologists.

The Role of Spore Prints in Mushroom Identification

Spore prints are a critical tool for distinguishing between edible and poisonous mushroom species. For example, the edible Agaricus campestris has a brown spore print, while the toxic look-alike Amanita virosa has a white spore print. For many mushrooms, spore color is a defining characteristic used in field guides and identification keys. It's one of the first features that mycologists and experienced foragers check.

Verification of Field Observations

Sometimes, mushrooms can appear very similar based on the cap, stem, and gill characteristics alone. A spore print can serve as a confirmatory test to validate or refute an initial identification based on macroscopic features.

Why They're a Crucial Tool for Foragers

Foragers cannot afford to make mistakes. Consuming a misidentified mushroom can lead to severe illness or death. Spore prints, being a straightforward and highly reliable method, are an indispensable tool in a forager's toolkit. They provide a level of confidence that is essential when foraging for food in the wild.

Making a spore print is like unveiling a secret message from the mushroom. It's a simple process but one that yields vital information for the safe and responsible foraging of wild mushrooms. As we have seen, the steps are easy to follow, and the rewards are great—a deeper connection with the fungi we encounter and the peace of mind that comes with accurate identification.

Conclusion

In this chapter, we embarked on a comprehensive journey through the world of psilocybin mushrooms, starting with an introduction to the relevant families and genera that house these remarkable species. We explored the taxonomy of fungi, placing emphasis on key characteristics that define psilocybin mushrooms, and highlighted their global distribution and favored habitats. We delved into the detailed profiles of common psilocybin species, enriching our understanding of their identifying features, natural habitats, growth patterns, potency, and effects. Importantly, we also confronted the sobering reality of dangerous look-alike species. The stark comparisons made between these deceptive mushrooms and their psilocybin counterparts underlined the critical importance of accurate identification, emphasizing the grave risks of poisoning that accompany misidentification. Lastly, we were armed with a practical, hands-on tool—spore printing. Through this guide, we learned how to create and interpret these prints, cementing their role as a vital asset in the forager's toolkit. As we close this chapter, the overarching message is clear: While the world of psilocybin mushrooms is rich and fascinating, meticulous and informed identification is the non-negotiable foundation for safe and responsible engagement with these potent fungi.

Chapter 5
Basic Mycology and Mushroom Life Cycle

Have you ever paused on a woodland walk to marvel at the intricate network of mushrooms poking through the leaf litter? Or, perhaps, you've recoiled in surprise as a cluster of fungi appears overnight on your lawn after heavy rain. Mushrooms are nature's enigmatic storytellers, popping up in all sorts of places, capturing our imagination and curiosity.

At the heart of these marvels is a deeply fascinating journey —one that is ancient, rhythmic, and largely unseen. Far from being simple, the life of a mushroom follows a captivating cycle punctuated by periods of growth, dormancy, and regeneration. It's a story that is both complex and mesmerizing, unfolding beneath our feet and hidden from plain sight.

Most of us are acquainted with mushrooms only when they appear above ground, their caps and stems on full display. Yet, this is but a brief chapter in their tale. The world of fungi stretches far beyond what meets the eye, and in this chapter, we will delve into the intricate ballet of the mushroom life cycle, from spore to mature fruiting body. By understanding the biology and behaviors of these captivating organisms, we not only gain insight into a hidden world, but we also come to appreciate the deep connections fungi forge with the ecosystems around them.

And, as we venture deeper, we'll discover the mysteries of certain mushrooms, like the psilocybin varieties. What roles do their psychedelic compounds play in the grand dance of their life cycle? What sets them apart from the rest? This chapter beckons you on a journey, one that promises a deeper understanding of these enigmatic beings that share our world. So, let's embark on this exploration together and uncover the secrets that lie beneath the forest floor and within the gills and caps of these remarkable organisms.

Introduction to the Kingdom of Fungi

One of the wonders of nature is the kingdom of Fungi, an intricate and diverse world that often goes unnoticed. When you think of fungi, mushrooms might be the first things that come to mind. However, fungi have a much broader presence, from the mold on expired bread to the yeast that gives bread its fluffy texture. So, what sets fungi apart from plants, animals, and other organisms?

Firstly, unlike green plants, fungi don't photosynthesize. Plants have chlorophyll that helps them convert sunlight into food, but fungi lack this pigment. Instead, they're decomposers, breaking down organic material to obtain their nutrients. Secondly, fungi are not like animals because they have cell walls. But these aren't the cellulose-rich walls of plants. Fungi possess walls made of chitin, the same material found in insect exoskeletons. This makes them uniquely resilient and different from both plants and animals.

The Structure of Fungal Cells

Delving deeper into fungi reveals a network of structures that are marvels of nature:

Hyphae

Think of hyphae as the building blocks of fungi. These are long, thin, and thread-like structures. Individual hyphae might seem unassuming, but when they intertwine, they form a powerful and efficient network.

Mycelium

This is the next level of organization. When hyphae collectively grow and spread, they create a web known as mycelium. If you've ever lifted a decaying log and noticed a white, web-like structure beneath, you've encountered mycelium. This structure serves as the main body of the fungus and is responsible for absorbing nutrients.

Chitin Cell Walls

Unlike the cell walls of plants made from cellulose, fungal cell walls contain chitin. This robust material provides not only strength but also flexibility. It's what makes fungi adaptable and resilient in various environments.

Fungal Reproduction

The world of fungal reproduction is a tale of intrigue. Fungi have evolved various means to ensure their survival and proliferation, employing both sexual and asexual methods:

Asexual Reproduction

This is a quick and efficient way for fungi to spread. Here, spores play a crucial role. Spores are to fungi as seeds are to plants. When conditions are right, fungi release spores which then disperse. These spores can survive harsh conditions, and when they find a suitable environment, they germinate and grow into new fungi. Molds and yeasts are prolific examples of fungi that reproduce asexually.

Sexual Reproduction

This process is more complex and involves the fusion of specialized structures from two different fungi. When these structures merge, they form a zygote which eventually develops into spores. These spores, when released, grow into fungi that have a combination of traits from both parent fungi. This method enhances genetic diversity and adaptability.

The Life Cycle of a Typical Mushroom

Mushrooms, the umbrella-like structures that pop up on lawns or woods, are the fruiting bodies of certain fungi. Their primary purpose? Spore production and dispersal. Here's a step-by-step look at their life cycle:

Spore Germination

Their journey begins with a spore released from a mature mushroom. Landing in a suitable environment, this spore germinates, giving rise to a tiny hyphal thread.

Mycelial Growth

As the hyphae grow, they branch out and form an expanding web—the mycelium. This network feeds on organic matter in the substrate, be it soil, wood, or another organic medium.

Formation of a Fruiting Body

Under the right conditions, which could be influenced by factors like temperature, moisture, and nutrient availability, the mycelium aggregates and differentiates to form the fruiting body—the mushroom we're familiar with.

Spore Release

The mature mushroom releases spores from structures called gills or pores, depending on the species. These spores are then dispersed by wind, water, or other agents, and the cycle begins anew.

Fungi are remarkable organisms with a myriad of forms and functions. From decomposing organic matter to partnering with plants in symbiotic relationships, they are indispensable components of our ecosystems. Their unique biology, which is so distinct from plants and animals, underscores the vast diversity of life on our planet. Whether you're marveling at a mushroom on a woodland walk or watching mold take over a slice of old bread, you're witnessing the wonders of the fungal kingdom in action.

The Magic of Mycology

The Majestic Journey of Mushrooms

Mushrooms, the often overlooked citizens of the forest floor, have a life cycle as fascinating and intricate as any tale of metamorphosis. From their inception as spores to their growth as mature fruiting bodies, the story of the mushroom is a dance of resilience, transformation, and survival.

The Start of a Grand Journey

The tale of a mushroom begins with a spore, a microscopic particle that holds the potential of an entire mushroom community within its tiny confines. These spores, each one smaller than a speck of dust, possess genetic information ready to develop into a full-fledged fungus. Imagine the spore as a dormant seed with dreams of grandeur. Once it lands in a suitable environment—perhaps a moist patch of soil or a decaying piece of wood—this dream begins to take shape.

From Spore to Mycelium

The spore germinates, giving birth to thin, hair-like structures called hyphae. As these hyphae grow, they intertwine and fuse, forming a vast, branching network known as the mycelium. This is the silent worker behind the scenes, diligently colonizing substrates, absorbing nutrients, and laying the foundation for future mushrooms.

The mycelium operates like nature's internet. Through it, nutrients are transferred, signals are exchanged, and a foundation is laid for future growth. The mycelium is the true body of the fungus, working diligently below the surface, while the mushroom—the fruiting body—is merely the reproductive organ.

The Formation of the Fruiting Body

The transition from mycelium to the fruiting body is one of nature's wonders. Triggered by environmental factors, such as light, temperature shifts, and perhaps even the sheer will to reproduce, the mycelium begins to form structures called hyphal knots. This is where the real magic happens. These knots then develop into primordia, the earliest recognizable form of what we know as mushrooms. Affectionately termed "pins" in the world of mycology, these baby mushrooms are a testament to the miraculous journey from spore to mushroom.

As the pins continue their growth, factors like humidity and temperature play a crucial role. Before long, these pins evolved, displaying the familiar structure of stem, cap, and gills.

The Mushroom's Anatomy

At a closer glance, the mushroom is an architectural marvel. The cap acts as an umbrella, sheltering the delicate gills beneath. These gills are the spore-producing factories of the mushroom. Some species possess a protective "veil," which, as the mushroom matures, breaks to reveal these gills.

The stem, apart from providing support, may house a ring—a remnant of the protective veil. This stem, like a proud pillar, elevates the cap, ensuring the efficient dispersal of spores.

The Circle of Life

The gills, now exposed, are ready to release their treasure: the spores. In a mesmerizing display, countless spores, each a potential new life, are released, sometimes appearing like ethereal wisps of smoke. These spores are nature's parachuters. Carried by the wind, they travel far and wide, crossing forests, valleys, and even continents.

This miraculous journey from a tiny, invisible spore to a majestic mushroom and back to a spore is a testament to the wonders of nature. Each stage—each transformation—is a chapter in the age-old saga of life, resilience, and rebirth. The next time you come across a mushroom in your path, remember you're witnessing the final act in a grand play of evolution and survival.

The Unique Biological Aspects of Psilocybin Mushrooms

Magic mushrooms, more technically known as psilocybin mushrooms, have a rich tapestry of history, mysticism, and science intertwined. While these mushrooms have been a part of Indigenous practices for thousands of years, they have gained recent attention for their potentially therapeutic applications. Let's dive into the fascinating world of these fungi, examining their biological traits, the purpose of their psychoactive components, and how they differ from their non-psychedelic counterparts.

Where and How Psilocybin and Psilocin are Produced in the Mushroom?

Psilocybin and psilocin are the primary psychoactive compounds found in magic mushrooms. These chemicals are what make someone experience hallucinations and altered states of consciousness when they consume these mushrooms.

These compounds are synthesized within the mushroom cells through a complex biosynthetic pathway. Enzymes, which are essentially nature's little chemists, transform a compound called tryptophan (which is an amino acid commonly found in many organisms) into psilocybin and psilocin. This process is somewhat akin to how plants produce alkaloids or essential oils, but the enzymes and pathways are unique to psilocybin-producing mushrooms.

Interestingly, not all parts of the mushroom contain equal concentrations of these psychoactive compounds. The cap of the mushroom typically has a higher concentration than the stem. It's also worth noting that these concentrations can vary greatly from one mushroom to another, even within the same species or batch.

The Biological Purpose of Psilocybin in Mushrooms

So, why do mushrooms produce psilocybin? This question has puzzled scientists for quite some time. Unlike thorns on a rose or toxins in a poison dart frog, the hallucinogenic properties of psilocybin don't seem to offer an immediately obvious benefit for the mushroom's survival.

One leading theory proposes that psilocybin acts as a deterrent for predators. Just as some plants have evolved spicy capsaicin to deter herbivores, mushrooms might produce hallucinogens to confuse or deter creatures that might want to snack on them. After all, a disoriented insect or small mammal might be less likely to return to a psychedelic food source.

Another theory, albeit a more speculative one, suggests that the presence of psilocybin might give these mushrooms an edge in the fierce competition for decomposing organic matter. Perhaps the altered state of consciousness in animals might lead to behaviors that aid the dispersion or life cycle of the mushroom.

What's clear is that more research is required to truly understand the evolutionary advantage, if any, that psilocybin provides to these mushrooms.

Differences Between Psilocybin Mushrooms and Other Mushrooms

With over 200 species of magic mushrooms, their diversity is rich, yet they also possess common characteristics that differentiate them from other fungi.

Growth Habits and Habitat Preferences

Psilocybin mushrooms tend to flourish in specific habitats. Many species prefer the dung of herbivores, particularly in grassy fields, making cow pastures a hotspot. Others might grow on decaying wood or in rich, organic soils. While other mushrooms might also grow in these conditions, the specific preferences of psilocybin mushrooms can sometimes be a clue to their identification.

Bruising

One unique characteristic of many (but not all) psilocybin-containing mushrooms is that they bruise blue when damaged. This is due to the oxidation of psilocin. However, it's essential to approach this trait with caution, as other non-psychedelic mushrooms can also exhibit blue bruising.

Physical Appearance

While many species of magic mushrooms look alike, making them difficult to distinguish, they can also closely resemble other non-psychedelic and even toxic mushrooms. This poses risks to foragers who might mistakenly consume a poisonous variety.

In summary, psilocybin mushrooms are a captivating blend of ancient lore and modern science. Their unique biological characteristics, from the synthesis of mind-altering compounds to their distinct growth habits, set them apart in the fungal kingdom. As we continue to explore their potential therapeutic applications, it's equally important to appreciate and respect their intricate nature and the mysteries they still hold.

Conclusion

In Chapter 5, we delved deep into the mesmerizing world of fungi, demystifying the key distinctions that set them apart from plants and animals. By understanding the intricacies of fungal cells—from the interconnected networks of hyphae and mycelium to their robust chitin cell walls—we gain a clearer picture of their life and vitality. The chapter meticulously guided the reader through the intricate dance of fungal reproduction, both sexual and asexual, and the ensuing journey of a mushroom's life, from the germination of a lone spore to the emergence of a mature fruiting body. We also took a closer look at the psilocybin mushroom, shining a light on its unique biological attributes, including the production of its potent compounds and its distinctive growth patterns. This exploration not only offers a comprehensive understanding of mushroom biology but also sets the stage for further appreciation of their ecological and cultural significance.

Chapter 6
Materials and Conditions for Growing

Have you ever tried assembling a jigsaw puzzle with a few missing pieces? Frustrating, isn't it? Just like that puzzle, cultivating perfect growth requires every piece in its place– from the tangible materials to the precise conditions. Without the right tools or the correct ambiance, your effort can feel like a puzzle forever incomplete. While the art of cultivation might seem intricate, once you grasp the importance of each component, the process transforms from puzzling to fascinating.

Imagine for a moment that you're holding in your hands a container rich with substrate, ready to be inoculated with spores. With each stage, from the moment you introduce those spores to when you marvel at the fruiting bodies, you are both an artist and a scientist. It's not merely about planting and waiting; it's about understanding, nurturing, and optimizing.

Materials, much like ingredients in a recipe, can make or break your cultivation journey. From the simplicity of containers and sterilization tools to the nuanced choice of spores or mycelium, every item you select will influence your end result. Some might get away with an off-brand alternative, while others might find the premium choice to be a game-changer. And while materials lay the foundation, it's the environment that acts as the nurturing mother. Like a plant that needs the perfect blend of sunlight, water, and soil nutrients, each stage of growth comes with its unique needs.

Of course, the world of fungi isn't one-size-fits-all. The psilocybin family alone is a diverse group, with siblings demanding their distinct care routines. Some might bask in the glory of direct sunlight, while others may shy away, preferring the cool embrace of the shadows. Recognizing the signs, both thriving and wilting, becomes paramount.

Join me as we embark on this illuminating voyage, diving deep into the world of cultivation. Whether you're an enthusiast seeking to understand the intricacies or a seasoned cultivator aiming to perfect the craft, this chapter promises a wealth of knowledge. Let's piece together this intricate jigsaw, ensuring that every piece finds its rightful place.

Required Materials for Mushroom Cultivation

Mushroom cultivation is a fascinating journey into the world of fungi, where with the right tools and knowledge, you can produce everything from simple edible varieties to intricate exotic species. This guide provides an in-depth look into the essential materials required for successful cultivation.

Containers

Containers are the backbone of your cultivation setup. They are the physical space where your mushrooms will sprout and flourish. Whether it's a plastic tote, a glass jar, or specialized mushroom bags, these vessels hold the substrate, offering the mushrooms an environment that helps control moisture, temperature, and potential contamination. If you could visualize it, you'd see a transparent container, tiny ventilation holes punctuating its sides, filled with substrate, with the early tendrils of white mycelium beginning their expansive journey. Brands like Sterilite and Rubbermaid are often favored for their durability. However, for those on a budget, repurposed food containers can work wonders. Ensure whatever you choose can be sealed and is easy to sterilize.

Substrate Materials

Substrate materials are the very sustenance for your fungi. This is what the mycelium, the vegetative part of the mushroom, consumes and derives its nutrients from. Depending on the type of mushroom you're growing, you might find yourself using brown rice flour, vermiculite, or even wood chips. Imagine slicing a container in half, revealing layers of this earthy material, the playground for the mycelium to weave through and consume. Recognized brands in this space include Hoffman's for vermiculite and Bob's Red Mill for organic brown rice flour. A cost-saving tip: Local agricultural stores or nurseries can be a treasure trove, offering bulk substrate materials at a fraction of the cost.

Spores

The magic truly begins with spores or mycelium. Think of spores as the seeds from which mushrooms sprout. They're microscopic, and when introduced to the right environment, they germinate and give rise to mycelium. You can also start your cultivation directly with mycelium, usually inoculated on grains, giving you a slight edge since it's already in a growth phase. Visualize a microscopic dark speck—that's your spore. And next to it, white, root-like structures enveloping grains—that's mycelium. Quality is paramount here. Brands like Sporeworks and MycoSupply are renowned for their spore syringes and grain spawn. As you progress in your mushroom journey, consider making your own spore prints or grain spawn, a great way to save money and become self-sufficient.

Sterilization Equipment

Last but certainly not least is the sterilization equipment. It's a non-negotiable in the world of mushroom cultivation. Given the sensitive nature of the process, any contaminants can be disastrous, ruining your entire batch. This is where equipment like pressure cookers comes into play, ensuring every tool and material you use is free from unwanted microorganisms. Picture a robust pressure cooker on a stovetop, steam spiraling out, with glass jars lined beside, freshly sterilized and awaiting their role. Presto and All American are brands that mushroom enthusiasts often swear by for their reliability. However, if you're trying to keep costs down, a large pot with a tight-fitting lid might suffice for steam sterilization, though be warned, it's not always as effective.

In summary, mushroom cultivation is akin to a well-orchestrated dance, with each material playing a pivotal role in the grand performance. From the humble container that houses the fungi to the spores that instigate life, understanding and choosing the right tools is integral. As you embark on or continue this mycological adventure, remember that with the right materials and a dash of patience, a bountiful harvest awaits.

Creating the Perfect Environment for Each Stage

Mushroom cultivation is a rewarding pursuit that can be approached both by enthusiasts and commercial growers alike. By following a few key practices, you can successfully navigate the different stages of mushroom growth, from germination to fruiting body maturation. In this guide, we'll cover the environmental requirements and best practices for each stage of mushroom growth.

Germination Stage

Preparing the Substrate

The substrate is the material on which mushrooms grow, and it acts as a source of nutrients for the developing fungi. There are many substrate options to choose from, including straw, wood chips, or a mixture of organic materials. Your choice of substrate should be based on the type of mushrooms you're cultivating and their specific needs.

Choose a suitable substrate

Start by selecting a substrate that matches the nutritional requirements of your chosen mushroom variety. For example, oyster mushrooms prefer straw, while shiitake mushrooms prefer hardwood chips.

Prepare the substrate

Cut or break down your substrate into smaller pieces, making it easier for the mushroom mycelium to colonize. For straw, cut it into 2–4 inch pieces. For wood chips, use small to medium-sized chips.

Moisten the substrate

Hydration is crucial at this stage. Moisten your substrate with water until it reaches the right moisture level (generally 60–75% water content by weight). You can achieve this by soaking, spraying, or mixing water with the substrate.

Sterilize the substrate

To prevent contamination from other microorganisms, sterilize your substrate by baking, pressure cooking, or pasteurizing it. For example, you can pressure cook the substrate at 15 psi for 90 minutes. Once sterilized, let the substrate cool before inoculation.

Inoculation

Inoculation is the process of introducing mushroom spores or mycelium into the substrate. You can use spore syringes, liquid culture, or grain spawn for inoculation.

Work in a Clean Environment

Minimize contamination risks by working in a clean and sanitized area. Wipe surfaces with isopropyl alcohol, and consider wearing gloves and a face mask.

Inoculate the Substrate

Introduce the spores or mycelium into the substrate by evenly distributing the inoculant throughout the substrate. For example, you can inject spore solution into the substrate using a syringe or mix grain spawn with the substrate.

Seal the Containers

After inoculation, seal the containers (e.g., bags or jars) with a breathable filter to allow gas exchange while preventing contamination.

Creating a Sterile Environment

Mushroom germination requires a clean environment free from competing microorganisms. Here are some tips to achieve this:

- Use a Still Air Box or Glove Box: These boxes are designed to reduce air currents, making it easier to work in a sterile environment.
- Keep the Inoculated Containers in a Clean Area: Store the containers in a dedicated space with minimal contamination risk, such as a clean room or designated incubation area.
- Monitor for Contamination: Check the containers regularly for signs of contamination, such as unusual colors, textures, or odors. If you suspect contamination, discard the affected substrate to prevent it from spreading to other containers.

Mycelial Growth Stage

During the mycelial growth stage, mushroom mycelium colonizes the substrate and prepares for fruiting body formation. Proper temperature, humidity, and light exposure are essential for optimal mycelial growth.

Temperature Control

Maintain a temperature range that supports mycelial growth. Generally, a temperature of 70–75°F (21–24°C) is suitable for most mushroom varieties. Use a thermostat and heater to regulate temperature, and avoid temperature fluctuations that may stress the mycelium.

Humidity

High humidity levels are crucial for mycelial growth. Maintain a relative humidity of 90–95% in the incubation area. Use a humidifier or manually mist the area with water to maintain the appropriate humidity levels.

Light Exposure

Mushroom mycelium does not require light for growth. However, some ambient light is beneficial for maintaining a regular growth cycle. Use indirect, natural light or low-intensity artificial light to provide a consistent light-dark cycle.

Preventing Contamination

- Excessive airflow can introduce contaminants. Minimize drafts and air currents in the incubation area.
- Regularly clean and sanitize the incubation area, equipment, and tools.
- Inspect the containers for signs of contamination, and take action if needed.

Formation and Maturation of Fruiting Bodies

The formation and maturation of fruiting bodies are the final stages of mushroom growth (Beyer, 2022). Here's how to optimize the conditions for these stages:

Temperature and Humidity

- Lower the Temperature: Reduce the temperature to 55–70°F (13–21°C) to encourage fruiting body formation.
- Adjust Humidity: Maintain a relative humidity of 85–90%. Use a humidifier or manually mist the area to achieve the desired humidity levels.

Light Exposure

Increase light exposure to stimulate fruiting body formation. Provide 12–16 hours of indirect, natural light, or use artificial light with a color temperature of 5,000–6,500 Kelvin.

Fresh Air Exchange

- Mushrooms produce carbon dioxide during growth and require fresh air exchange to thrive. Use a fan or open windows to increase airflow, ensuring that CO_2 levels stay low and oxygen levels remain high.
- As you increase airflow, the substrate may dry out. Maintain moisture levels by misting the substrate with water.

Harvesting

Monitor for Maturity

Harvest mushrooms when the caps have fully expanded but before the spores drop. For most varieties, this is when the edges of the caps start to turn upward.

Harvest Gently

Twist or cut the mushrooms gently at the base, taking care not to damage the substrate.

Creating the perfect environment for each stage of mushroom growth requires attention to detail, careful monitoring, and the right equipment. By following these guidelines, you can successfully cultivate healthy, abundant mushrooms at home or on a commercial scale. Happy mushroom growing!

Specific Temperature, Humidity, and Light Requirements for Different Species

When cultivating mushrooms, it is important to note that different species have different environmental requirements for optimal growth. These requirements can differ significantly among various mushroom species, especially in terms of temperature, humidity, and light exposure. To successfully cultivate different species of mushrooms, it is essential to tailor the growing conditions to meet the specific needs of each species. Below, we will examine some of these differences and provide detailed profiles of a few common psilocybin species and their cultivation requirements.

Examination of Different Environmental Needs

Temperature

Most mushrooms have an ideal temperature range for mycelial growth and fruiting body formation. This range varies across species and can also differ between the mycelial and fruiting stages of the same species. For example, some tropical mushroom varieties prefer higher temperatures, while others thrive in cooler environments.

Humidity

Like temperature, humidity levels need to be adjusted depending on the species and growth stage. In general, mushroom mycelium requires high humidity levels during colonization, while fruiting bodies may require slightly lower humidity levels.

Light Exposure

Light requirements vary among mushroom species. Some mushrooms grow well in low light conditions, while others require exposure to light for the formation and development of fruiting bodies. Light exposure can also impact the size, shape, and color of the mushrooms.

Profiles of Common Psilocybin Species

Psilocybe Cubensis

- Temperature: For mycelial growth, maintain a temperature of 75–80°F (24–27°C). For fruiting, a slightly lower temperature of 74–78°F (23–26°C) is ideal (Hoa & Wang, 2015).
- Humidity: Maintain a relative humidity of 90–95% during colonization and reduce it to 85–90% during fruiting.
- Light Exposure: Provide indirect, natural light or low-intensity artificial light for 12–16 hours a day to stimulate fruiting.

Psilocybe Cyanescens

- Temperature: This species prefers cooler temperatures. Keep it between 65–75°F (18–24°C) for mycelial growth and 50–60°F (10–16°C) for fruiting.
- Humidity: Maintain a relative humidity of 90–95% during colonization and reduce it to 85–90% during fruiting.

- Light Exposure: Provide indirect, natural light or low-intensity artificial light for 12–16 hours a day to stimulate fruiting.

Psilocybe Semilanceata (Liberty Caps)

- Temperature: The optimal temperature for mycelial growth is 70–75°F (21–24°C), while for fruiting, it's 60–70°F (16–21°C).
- Humidity: Maintain a relative humidity of 90–95% during colonization and reduce it to 85–90% during fruiting.
- Light Exposure: Provide indirect, natural light, or low-intensity artificial light for 12–16 hours a day to stimulate fruiting.

Adjusting Growing Conditions

Adjusting Conditions

Be prepared to adjust the growing conditions as needed based on the species' requirements and their reactions to the environment. You may need to change temperature, humidity, or light levels if you notice signs of unhealthy growth.

Signs of Healthy Growth

Healthy mycelium appears as a thick, white, cottony layer. Fruiting bodies should be well-formed, firm, and free from abnormalities. In the case of psilocybin mushrooms, they should have a characteristic blue bruising when handled.

Signs of Unhealthy Growth

Indicators of unhealthy growth include slow colonization, uneven mycelial growth, or the presence of other colors in the mycelium, which could be signs of contamination. Fruiting bodies that are misshapen, discolored, or have a slimy texture may be unhealthy or contaminated.

Cultivating different species of mushrooms requires an understanding of the specific temperature, humidity, and light requirements of each species. Tailoring the growing environment to meet these needs is crucial for optimal growth. By closely monitoring your mushrooms and being prepared to adjust conditions as needed, you can achieve successful cultivation and enjoy the unique and fascinating world of mushrooms.

Conclusion

In Chapter 6, we have explored the essential materials and conditions necessary for successful mushroom cultivation. We have provided a comprehensive list of required materials, from containers and substrates to spores or mycelium and sterilization equipment. We have explained the purpose of each material and offered recommendations for sourcing, brand selection, and cost-saving alternatives. Additionally, we have delved into the specific environmental requirements for each stage of mushroom growth, from germination and mycelial growth to the formation and maturation of fruiting bodies. We have outlined the crucial factors of temperature control, humidity, light exposure, and contamination prevention. Lastly, we have discussed the importance of tailoring growing conditions to meet the specific needs of different mushroom species. By understanding and adapting to the unique requirements of each species, cultivators can optimize growth and enjoy a fruitful harvest of psilocybin mushrooms. The knowledge and recommendations in this chapter serve as a valuable guide for both novice and experienced mushroom cultivators.

Chapter 7
Cultivation Process

Imagine, for a moment, walking into an artist's studio. Pots of paint lay scattered, brushes of various sizes lined up, and a blank canvas positioned on the easel. The potential is palpable, and every element plays its part. Much like an artist preparing for a masterpiece, mushroom cultivation is a blend of science, art, and patience.

Behind the scenes of every delicious or therapeutic mushroom is an intricate dance of details and steps that lead to the glorious finale, from the all-important base where these fungi find their grounding—the substrate—to the careful methods of keeping things pure and uncontaminated, every decision counts.

Consider the substrate as our canvas. It's the base where the magic begins, with myriad choices, each holding its unique attributes. But a canvas alone doesn't make art. The sterilization methods are the brushes, ensuring each stroke is clean, precise, and free from unwanted splatters.

Once everything is set, we introduce life, the "paint"—this is where inoculation comes in, allowing the mycelium to dance across its canvas. The care, the adjustments, the keen eye—it's a tender relationship between the cultivator and the growing mycelium.

As time progresses, cues from the environment beckon the masterpiece to reveal itself: the fruiting phase. Like finishing touches, knowing when and how to encourage the mushroom to emerge and when to harvest requires both knowledge and intuition.

But, as with all art, challenges arise. Mistakes can happen. A blob of unwanted paint, an unexpected smear. Yet, even these can be addressed, corrected, or sometimes even incorporated to make the end result even better.

In this chapter, we delve into this beautiful ballet of mushroom cultivation. You'll discover the nuances, the techniques, and the insights to transform your cultivation experience from mere science to art. Ready to paint your masterpiece? Let's begin.

Preparing Your Substrate

Cultivating mushrooms isn't just about spores, humidity, and light; the substrate you choose plays a pivotal role. Think of the substrate as the canvas upon which an artist paints. The right substrate provides essential nutrients and sets the stage for the mushroom mycelium to grow, colonize, and eventually produce fruiting bodies. Let's deep dive into the role of substrate, explore various options, and walk you through a detailed guide on preparing the best substrate for your mushrooms.

The Role of Substrate in Mushroom Cultivation

Nurturing Ground for Mycelium

Mushrooms, unlike plants, don't have chlorophyll to produce their own food. Instead, they rely on external materials, mainly the substrate, to provide necessary nutrients. It's within the substrate that the mushroom mycelium—the root-like structure of fungi—spreads, consumes, and establishes a strong network.

Maintaining Optimal Moisture

A well-prepared substrate retains just the right amount of moisture. This hydration is critical for mushroom development. Too dry, and the mycelium can't expand. It's too wet, and it's a breeding ground for contaminants.

Creating the Perfect Environment

Beyond nutrients and moisture, substrates help maintain pH balance, buffer against environmental changes, and provide the necessary structure for mushrooms to anchor and grow.

A Breakdown of Different Substrate Options

Selecting the right substrate is akin to choosing the perfect soil for your plants. It's the bedrock of mushroom cultivation. While the overarching goal is to provide a nutritious haven for mycelium growth, not all substrates are created equal. Each comes with its own set of benefits and drawbacks, and the choice often depends on the mushroom species you're cultivating. Let's delve into the specifics.

Brown Rice Flour (BRF) and Vermiculite Mix

- **Pros**

Beginner-Friendly: This combination is straightforward with easily accessible ingredients, making it a favorite among novice mushroom cultivators.

Versatility: Suitable for a variety of mushroom species, especially when employing the PF Tek method.

Texture and Airflow: Vermiculite aids in retaining moisture while providing good airflow, which is essential for healthy mycelium growth.

- **Cons**

Limited Nutrient Content: Compared to other substrates, BRF may not offer the most nutrients for some demanding species.

Scale Limitation: While ideal for small-scale cultivation, it's not the most efficient for larger or bulk operations.

Wood Chips or Sawdust

- **Pros**

Natural Environment: Many mushrooms, especially Shiitake and Oyster, naturally grow on wood, making this an ideal substrate.

Long-Term Cultivation: Wood chips can support multiple flushes or harvests.

Outdoor Options: Suitable for creating outdoor mushroom beds or patches.

- **Cons**

Supplementation: To achieve optimal yields, additional nutrients might be needed.

Species Restriction: Not every mushroom species thrives on wood. Some, like the Agaricus family, need different nutrients.

Straw

- **Pros**

Economical: Straw is often cheap and widely available.

Bulk Cultivation: Given its affordability and ease of preparation, straw works well for larger harvests.

Structure: Provides good aeration and structure for mushrooms to anchor and grow.

- **Cons**

Contamination Risk: Straw can be a hotspot for mold and other unwanted organisms if not properly pasteurized.

Preparation Time: It requires chopping, wetting, and pasteurizing before it's ready for inoculation.

Manure-based Substrates (e.g., Horse or Cow Manure)

- **Pros**

Rich Nutrient Profile: Manure is packed with nutrients, which can lead to abundant yields.

Mimics Natural Environment: Many mushrooms, like Psilocybe cubensis, naturally grow in or near dung in the wild.

Supports Multiple Flushing: The nutrient richness can support multiple harvests.

- **Cons**

Odor: Working with manure means dealing with a potent smell.

Higher Contamination Risk: Given its organic richness, it can attract various contaminants if not sterilized properly.

Compost

- **Pros**

Nutrient Dense: Well-decomposed compost offers a buffet of nutrients for mycelium.

Eco-friendly: Making use of kitchen waste and yard trimmings is a sustainable option.

Versatility: Suitable for various mushroom species due to its broad nutrient profile.

- **Cons**

Time-Consuming: Creating quality compost takes time, sometimes weeks or months.

Potential Contaminants: If the compost isn't properly decomposed or is made from contaminated materials, it can introduce unwanted microbes to the mix.

By understanding the unique attributes of each substrate, cultivators can optimize their growing conditions. The perfect substrate doesn't just nourish but also protects and supports the delicate mycelium as it works its magic. Your mushrooms are only as good as the foundation they grow on, so choose wisely!

Sterilization Methods in Mushroom Cultivation

Mushroom cultivation is both a science and an art. At the heart of this practice is the significance of sterilization. Sterilization acts as a shield, warding off unwanted contaminants that could otherwise wreak havoc on a mushroom grower's hard work. By understanding and mastering the various methods of sterilization, growers stand a better chance of achieving success in their cultivation journey.

Mushrooms, though enchanting and beneficial, are particularly sensitive to their environment. They thrive in a specific set of conditions, making them susceptible to contamination. Mold, bacteria, and other fungi are constantly in competition with mushroom mycelium. These microscopic invaders are voracious and can outpace and overshadow mushroom growth if given the slightest opportunity.

Moist, nutrient-rich substrates, the very environment mushrooms thrive in, are akin to an all-you-can-eat buffet for these unwanted organisms. Thus, sterilization is akin to setting a secure boundary, ensuring that your mushrooms have the best possible head start. Without it, the nutrient-dense environment you've created can quickly become a playground for contaminants.

Overview of Various Sterilization Methods

Mushroom sterilization is not a one-size-fits-all endeavor. Depending on the type of substrate, the specific mushroom strain, and even the equipment at hand, growers might opt for different sterilization methods. These methods can be broadly categorized into three types: pressure cooking, steam sterilization, and chemical sterilization.

Pressure Cooking

This method harnesses the power of temperature and pressure. By elevating the heat under controlled pressure, one can achieve temperatures beyond the boiling point of water, ensuring the death of most bacteria and spores.

Steam Sterilization

While it might sound similar to pressure cooking, steam sterilization, particularly atmospheric steam sterilization, doesn't rely on increased pressure. Instead, it utilizes prolonged exposure to high temperatures.

Chemical Sterilization

This is a more niche method, where chemicals are used to eliminate potential contaminants. While not as commonly used as the other methods, it does have its applications, especially in large-scale operations or in specific situations.

Detailed Guides for Each Method

Pressure Cooking

- **Overview**

Commonly used by small-scale mushroom growers, pressure cooking is the go-to method for many, especially those dealing with nutrient-rich substrates. This method uses specialized equipment, like pressure cookers or autoclaves, to achieve the desired sterilization effect.

Procedure

- **Equipment Needed**

You will need a pressure cooker or autoclave, jars or bags of your prepared substrate, a metal cooking rack, and water.

- Begin by checking your pressure cooker. Ensure seals are intact and all parts are in good condition.
- Before placing your substrate in the cooker, ensure the bags are folded correctly to prevent excessive steam from entering. If you're using jars, cover the filters with foil.

- Use a metal rack or jar lids at the base of the cooker to prevent direct contact of bags or jars with the cooker's base.
- Add water. The exact amount varies, but starting with about 3 quarts (2.8 liters) is a good baseline.
- Seal your cooker and set it on high heat. Once steam begins to vent steadily, place a 15 PSI pressure regulator on the vent.
- Once the desired pressure is achieved, lower the heat and maintain the pressure for the required duration, typically 1 to 4 hours, depending on the substrate volume.
- After sterilization, allow the substrate to cool in the cooker for at least 8 hours before inoculating.
- When to Use: Ideal for high-nutrient substrates like manure, grains, and master's mix. It's also best suited for small to medium-sized batches.

Steam Sterilization

- **Overview**

This method, particularly atmospheric steam sterilization, is excellent for larger batches or for those who do not have access to pressure cookers.

Procedure

- **Equipment Needed**

You will need a barrel steam sterilizer or a similar device, water, and your substrate in bags or containers.

- Place the substrate inside the steam sterilizer.
- The goal is to maintain temperatures between 194 and 212°F (90 and 100°C) for an extended period, sometimes up to 18 hours.
- After the cycle, allow the substrate to cool for several hours.
- When to Use: Perfect for less nutritious substrates, like straw or sugarcane bagasse. It's also suitable for larger batches that might not fit inside standard pressure cookers.

Chemical Sterilization

- **Overview**

This method is less common in small-scale mushroom cultivation but can be effective, especially when dealing with challenging contaminants or large-scale operations.

- **Procedure**

The specifics of chemical sterilization can vary based on the chemical in use and the substrate. Typically, the substrate is soaked or treated with a chemical solution that eliminates potential contaminants. After treatment, the substrate often needs thorough rinsing or a period of off-gassing to ensure no chemical residues remain.

- **When to Use**

This method is good to use in situations where other sterilization methods are ineffective or impractical. However, this method requires careful handling and knowledge of the chemicals involved.

Sterilization is the unsung hero of mushroom cultivation. It's the gatekeeper, ensuring that your hard work and dedication bear fruit—or, in this case, fungi. By understanding and choosing the right sterilization method, you not only protect your crop but also maximize its potential, leading to bountiful harvests and the joy of cultivation. Remember, in the world of mushrooms, cleanliness isn't just next to godliness; it's the pathway to success.

Procedures for Inoculation and Caring for the Mycelium During Colonization

Mushroom cultivation is an intricate and rewarding process. One of the most crucial stages is the inoculation of the substrate with mycelium. Properly understanding and executing this stage ensures a prolific harvest. Let's dive deep into this fascinating world of mushroom cultivation.

The Inoculation Process

Mushroom cultivation is an art, a science, and, for many, a passion. It mirrors the process of sowing seeds in a fertile garden, hoping for a bountiful harvest. However, instead of seeds, in mushroom cultivation, we introduce spores or mycelium into a carefully prepared substrate. This introduction, known as "inoculation," is a pivotal moment in the mushroom-growing journey. It sets the stage for the growth and eventual fruition of the mushroom. Getting the inoculation right can make the difference between a lush, flourishing mycelial network and a stalled growth or, worse, a contaminated substrate. This initial phase demands precision, cleanliness, and an understanding of the nuanced steps involved. Let's unravel this intricate process step by step, ensuring we lay a solid foundation for our mushroom cultivation endeavor.

Preparing the Inoculum

If using a liquid culture syringe, shaking it well is essential to ensure even distribution of mycelium. For those utilizing mycelium grown on agar, a sterilized scalpel should be used to cut a rice grain-sized piece. This little piece will be the "seed" for our mushroom cultivation.

Sterilization Is Key

Flame sterilization of your needle or scalpel ensures no contaminants are obliterated. The instrument should be heated until it glows red and then allowed to cool before use. This step ensures the only thing you're introducing to your substrate is the desired mycelium or spores.

The Act of Inoculation

If you're using a syringe, introduce it through the jar's self-healing injection port, injecting about 1–2 mL of the liquid culture into your broth. Using agar? Just open the lid slightly, slide the agar piece in, and seal immediately. Remember, this process should be swift to reduce contamination risks.

Distribution

After inoculation, a gentle shake of your broth helps distribute the mycelium uniformly throughout the liquid. Think of it as giving the mycelium a head start, ensuring it reaches all parts of the substrate.

Maintaining Optimal Conditions During Mycelial Colonization

Mycelial colonization is like the germination phase of plants. As the mycelium expands, it's important to offer it the best conditions:

Incubation

After inoculation, your jar needs a cozy, dark place to kick-start the growth. Depending on the mushroom type, room temperature is often ideal. However, always check for strain-specific temperature requirements.

Agitation and Oxygenation

As mycelium starts growing, agitation helps distribute it evenly. Shaking the jar containing a glass marble or using a magnetic stirrer ensures nutrients are consumed efficiently and results in a well-mixed liquid culture.

Monitoring and Care

Daily observation of your liquid culture is imperative. Cloudy white formations indicate mycelium growth, prompting the agitation process. And remember, while you want to shake or stir firmly, be gentle to avoid potential messes or damage.

Signs to Ensure the Mycelium is Healthy and Progressing

As with any cultivation process, signs of health and potential issues should always be on your radar.

Visual Indicators

Healthy mycelium appears as a white, web-like growth. As your inoculated substrate begins colonization, you should observe this white, thread-like expansion. It's a visual treat and an indicator of a thriving culture.

Watch Out for Contaminants

Not all growth is good. Colors like green or black are red flags. These indicate contamination, which can jeopardize your entire cultivation effort. Always be vigilant.

Progress and Expansion

The colonization of the substrate should be relatively consistent. Over days and weeks, the mycelium will fully occupy the substrate, preparing itself for fruiting. Regular checks ensure you're on the right track.

The journey of mushroom cultivation is a delicate dance between the cultivator and the fungi. From inoculation to watching the mycelium colonize the substrate, each step is crucial. As you delve deeper into this captivating world, remember the importance of sterility, care, and observation.

With patience and dedication, you'll soon witness the incredible world of mushrooms springing to life in your very own cultivation setup.

Tips for Encouraging Fruiting and Determining When to Harvest

Mushroom cultivation is not just about planting and waiting for the harvest. It's a delicate ballet of environmental controls, subtle cues, and instinctive adjustments. It requires patience, precision, and a keen eye. In this comprehensive guide, we'll delve into the intricacies of encouraging fruiting, identifying optimal harvest times, and ensuring the health and sustainability of the underlying mycelium.

The Fruiting Conundrum

Mushroom fruiting is the culmination of the fungus's life cycle, leading to the production of spores and ensuring the continuation of the species. Yet, what precisely kickstarts this phase? The answer lies in a symphony of environmental cues:

Light

Contrary to the common myth that mushrooms thrive in darkness, most specialty mushrooms require light to fruit optimally. Light seemingly acts as a measure, guiding the length of their stems. In insufficient lighting, mushrooms tend to grow skinny with elongated stems. Standard shop lights or energy-efficient LED strip lighting usually suffices for the mushroom's needs.

Temperature

Most mushroom species find the sweet spot for fruiting in the low 60s°F (around 62–65°F). A basement or an in-ground area can often provide this range without much need for heating or cooling. Temperatures below 50–55°F slow down fruiting, while above 75°F, they may yield low-quality mushrooms or decrease productivity.

Humidity

Freshly initiated mushrooms are vulnerable and need high humidity levels (above 85%). As they mature, they can withstand levels as low as 60%, but 80% is optimal. Humidity ensures the young mushroom pins develop properly and mature into juicy, full-bodied fruits.

Oxygen

Mushrooms respire, much like us, absorbing oxygen and releasing CO_2. Ensuring regular fresh air supply is crucial, with CO_2 levels ideally below 1000 PPM for most species. Oyster mushrooms prefer even lower levels, below 800 PPM. Regular air exchange rejuvenates the growing space and encourages healthy fruiting.

Create an Ideal Environment

Whether you choose a simple outdoor fruiting space or a highly controlled indoor setup, it's essential to constantly monitor temperature, humidity, lighting, and oxygen levels. Regular adjustments based on observations ensure optimal conditions for fruiting.

Shift Species Based on Seasons

Some mushrooms, like oysters, have variants suited to different temperatures. Shifting between Pleurotus ostreatus (for colder months) and Pleurotus pulmonarius (for warmer months) can optimize yields year-round.

Efficient Air Exchange

Instead of a constant low-level fan, consider using a stronger fan to rapidly exchange the air in short bursts. This method, coupled with simultaneous intake and exhaust fans, helps maintain desired oxygen levels without overburdening the cooling system.

Invest in Efficient Equipment

Commercial humidifiers, coupled with a humidistat or timer, help maintain ideal humidity levels. LED lighting, known for its energy efficiency, provides ample light without generating excess heat.

The Right Harvest Time and the Art of Picking

As much as triggering fruiting is an art, so is determining the perfect harvest time. Mushrooms communicate their needs and readiness through their morphology, color, texture, and overall abundance.

Visual Cues

Often, a mushroom nearing its harvest time will display distinct signs. The cap starts to uncurl, revealing the gills underneath. However, if the cap flattens entirely or turns upwards, it may be slightly overdue.

Texture

Mushrooms ready for harvesting will have a firm, meaty texture, neither too soggy nor too dry.

Harvesting Technique

Gently grip the mushroom at its base and twist it off without yanking. This method ensures the underlying mycelium isn't damaged, preserving it for potential future fruiting. Ensure hands are clean or use gloves to avoid contamination.

Mushroom cultivation, especially the fruiting phase, requires more than just technical knowledge. It demands intuition, built from careful observation and experience. As you embark on your mushroom-growing journey, remember that each batch teaches you something new. Whether it's a shift in environmental parameters, a nudge in lighting, or a variation in humidity, each adjustment brings you closer to mastering the art and science of mushroom cultivation. In the world of fungi, patience and attentiveness are the greatest allies.

Common Cultivation Issues in Mushroom Growth

Mushroom cultivation is an art, a science, and a little bit of magic. And as with all things, the journey to mastering it can sometimes be paved with obstacles. Yet, understanding the common pitfalls and knowing how to navigate around them can lead to a rewarding cultivation experience.

Contamination

Arguably the most prevalent problem, contamination usually arises from bacteria, molds, and other unwanted organisms. When they manifest, they can consume the nutrients meant for the mushroom mycelium, making the substrate unusable.

Poor or Slow Mycelial Growth

Mycelium, the root system of mushrooms, sometimes fails to thrive, leading to stunted growth or none at all.

Failure to Fruit

Sometimes, even if mycelium colonizes the substrate, the conditions might not be conducive for it to bear fruit.

Poor Yield

A poor yield is a scenario where the mushrooms grow but not in the abundance one might expect or hope for.

Now, let's delve into these problems and unravel the remedies.

Tackling Contamination

Causes: Contamination is chiefly due to improper sterilization. The culprits include inadequately sterilized equipment, containers, gloves, and substrates. A less-than-sterile environment further exacerbates this issue.

Solutions

Meticulous Sterilization: Every tool, surface, and material must be treated with the utmost care. Using a pressure cooker is recommended for heat sterilization, ensuring the pressure is consistently checked. Additionally, sterilize syringe needles and scalpels with a flame after each use when dealing with liquid cultures and agar.

Clean Workspace: A spick-and-span workspace is not just about aesthetics; it's a necessity. This decreases the chances of external contaminants infiltrating the cultivation process.

Ensuring Healthy Mycelial Growth

Causes: Impatience, primarily. Rushing through the cultivation process, not allowing substrates to cool before inoculation, or moving to the fruiting stage before complete colonization can hamper mycelial growth.

Solutions

Patience Is Virtue: Mushroom growth is not a sprint. It's a marathon. Every step should be performed with diligence and patience.

Adhere to Techniques: It's tempting to jump between methods, but consistency is key. Choose a technique and stick to it from beginning to end.

Encouraging Fruiting

Causes: The primary cause is not providing the right environment for the mycelium to fruit.

Solutions

Optimal Environment: Mushrooms are finicky about where they grow. Every strain has its own requirements concerning air and ground temperature, humidity, light conditions, and fresh air exchange. Research the specific needs of your chosen mushroom variety and replicate those conditions as closely as possible.

Avoid Over-Ambition: While enthusiasm is great, it's essential to grow at a pace that matches your resources and knowledge. Overextending can lead to failures.

Boosting Yield

Causes: A sub-optimal environment or substrate conditions can result in diminished yields.

Solutions

Mind the Thermogenesis: As mycelium breaks down organic matter, it generates heat—a phenomenon known as thermogenesis. This self-produced heat might cook and kill the mycelium. It's imperative to ensure that the substrate temperature remains optimal.

Substrate Consistency: An overly wet or dry substrate is detrimental. Aim for dampness—a gentle squeeze should only release a few droplets of water.

Additional Tips

- Early Detection: Familiarize yourself with how contaminations look in the early stages. Prompt detection can save resources.

- Labeling: This is a simple yet crucial step. Label jars with relevant details like species, date, and batch number.
- Post-Work Ventilation: Once you're done working with spores, ensure you ventilate your workspace to prevent any unwanted contaminants from settling.

Mushroom cultivation, like any craft, requires patience, precision, and persistence. While challenges are inevitable, they're also surmountable. With the right techniques, tools, and tenacity, you can navigate the intricate dance of mushroom cultivation and reap the delicious and perhaps magical rewards.

Conclusion

In this chapter, we journeyed through the intricate tapestry of mushroom cultivation, elucidating every step from substrate preparation to the eventual harvest. With a clear understanding of substrates' pivotal role and the myriad of options available, one can set a firm foundation for successful cultivation. The emphasis on rigorous sterilization processes underscores the necessity for an uncontaminated environment, which is vital for the thriving of mushrooms. Inoculation and the subsequent care of mycelium during colonization shape the trajectory of growth, with special cues and triggers paving the way for fruiting. While challenges in cultivation are par for the course, armed with the insights provided, cultivators are better equipped to troubleshoot issues and maximize their yield. As with all things worth pursuing, patience, knowledge, and attentive care remain the cornerstones of a prosperous mushroom cultivation journey.

Chapter 8
Safe Use and Maximizing Benefits

Imagine standing on the edge of a majestic cliff. Below, the azure waves of the ocean kiss the shores, and the winds carry the promises of adventure and discovery. But the breathtaking view comes with a warning: Without proper caution, that very edge can become perilous. The realm of psilocybin, with its kaleidoscope of sensory perceptions and deep introspective voyages, is no different than that cliff. When approached with respect, preparation, and a touch of awe, it can usher you into rooms of your mind you never knew existed, revealing profound truths and reshaping your understanding of reality.

But just as you wouldn't stand at the edge of a cliff without being mindful of your footing, you shouldn't dive into a psilocybin experience without adequate preparation. Dosage isn't merely a number—it's a key that can unlock doors of perception, influenced by factors like body weight, tolerance, and even the potency of different strains. The setting? It's not just about the ambiance of the room but the emotional and mental scenery you bring with you.

Picture preparing for a marathon. You wouldn't show up without having trained, both physically and mentally, would you? In the same way, psilocybin asks for your dedication. From dietary choices that prepare your body to intentions that guide your journey, every choice matters. Even once the journey concludes, the process is not truly over. Like an explorer documenting newfound territories, integration becomes the compass, ensuring the insights and revelations aren't fleeting but transform into actions that echo in the tangible world.

Ever heard of microdosing? It's the subtle art of using psilo-cybin in minute quantities—a whispered conversation with your psyche rather than a full-blown symposium. But even whispers carry weight, and understanding the how-tos and potential risks becomes essential.

In this chapter, think of me as your seasoned guide, one who has traversed these terrains and is equipped to lead you through its meandering paths. We'll delve into the intricacies of dosage, set the stage (quite literally) for your experience, guide you through physical and mental preparations, and show you how to navigate the often-overlooked yet crucial aftermath. In the end, like any great adventure, the voyage with psilocybin is as much about the journey as it is about the destination. So, strap in, open your heart and mind, and let's embark on this transformative expedition together.

Treading With Respect and Knowledge

In the vast, intricately woven tapestry of human experiences, psychedelics occupy a uniquely vivid and transformative corner. These substances have been present in human history for millennia, revered by Indigenous societies, pondered upon by philosophers, and, more recently, probed by scientists. For all their allure and promise, psychedelics are not toys to be trifled with. Their profound effects on consciousness, perception, and emotion can be both revelatory and destabilizing. Entering this realm without due preparation is akin to navigating uncharted waters without a compass. This guide, therefore, has been crafted to serve as that navigational tool, steering curious souls toward informed, safe, and enriching encounters with these powerful substances.

The Importance of Responsible Use, Safety, and Legality

Responsible Use

The renaissance of interest in psychedelics has been accompanied by numerous anecdotal accounts of transformative experiences, potential therapeutic benefits, and improved creativity. Yet, for all the mystique and promise, the line between enhancement and endangerment is slender.

Misuse can lead to unintended physical, psychological, and legal consequences. For instance, an excess dose might result in a traumatic experience, possibly causing long-lasting psychological distress.

Safety

When it comes to psychedelics, safety isn't just about the substance but also the sources. Consuming the wrong type of mushroom, for example, can be lethal. Therefore, ensure the provenance of the substance you are using, especially when dealing with naturally occurring psychedelics like mushrooms. It's not worth risking one's health or life.

Legality

Although there's a movement toward decriminalization, many psychedelic substances remain illegal in numerous jurisdictions. Being caught with such substances can have dire legal consequences. Always be aware of the laws in your location.

Calculating Dosage

Factors to Consider

Body Weight: Like many substances, body weight can influence how one might react to a dose.

Tolerance: If you've used psychedelics before, your tolerance might be higher, requiring a slightly larger dose for the same effect. Conversely, newcomers should start low.

Desired Effect: Microdosing, for instance, requires a subperceptual dose, not meant to induce hallucinations but to possibly enhance mood and creativity.

General Dosage Ranges

For psilocybin, anecdotal evidence suggests a medium-strength dose ranges between 2 to 3 grams of dried mushrooms, while a microdose is around 0.3 grams. However, the potency can vary drastically, making exact doses difficult (Grinspoon, 2022).

Adjusting Dosage Based on Potency

Different species or batches might have varying strengths. Thus, when trying a new batch or type, it's safer to start with a lower dose and gradually find what works for you.

Choosing a Safe and Comfortable Setting

Two primary elements influence a psychedelic experience: mindset and setting. Your psychological state (set) and physical surroundings (setting) can steer the journey in very different directions. Being in a safe, familiar, and comfortable environment is paramount.

Considerations for Company

Who you're with can significantly impact your experience. Trusted friends who either partake or remain sober can help guide the journey, ensuring safety and comfort. It's advisable to avoid mixing psychedelics with strangers or in unfamiliar settings.

As interest in psychedelics grows and new scientific investigations unfold, their potential and pitfalls become more evident. At the heart of this intricate dance is responsible use. Like the psilocybin mushrooms' mycelial network that stretches beneath the ground, a web of decisions and considerations lies beneath any psychedelic experience.

Physical Preparation for Psilocybin Experience

Embarking on a journey with psilocybin, whether for therapeutic reasons or personal exploration, requires more than just a decision. The experience, often described as profound and transformative, can be both exhilarating and daunting. Proper preparation can make the difference between a valuable, enlightening session and a challenging ordeal. From understanding the dietary prerequisites to anticipating the physical and sensory changes, every aspect plays a crucial role in shaping the journey.

Fasting

It is recommended that one should fast for at least six hours before taking psilocybin. This fasting period ensures an empty stomach, which can potentially enhance the absorption of psilocybin, making the experience more profound. Furthermore, fasting can also reduce the likelihood of nausea, a common side effect associated with psilocybin ingestion.

Foods to Avoid

When preparing for a psilocybin experience, steer clear of heavy, greasy, or spicy foods, as these might exacerbate feelings of nausea. Alcohol and caffeine should be minimized or entirely avoided, as they can alter the effects of psilocybin and add a layer of unpredictability.

Hydration

Staying well-hydrated is essential. While psilocybin itself doesn't dehydrate you, the experience can be physically taxing, and it's easy to forget basic necessities. Drinking water can also help flush out toxins and alleviate potential headaches.

What to Expect During the Experience

Venturing into the realm of psilocybin is akin to embarking on an uncharted journey where the landscape of one's mind unfolds in mysterious and unpredictable ways. Much like a traveler preparing for a voyage, it's invaluable to have a roadmap of what lies ahead. The experience can stretch the boundaries of perception, offering a spectrum of sensory changes and physical sensations, often following a discernible timeline.

Timeline of Effects

Onset: The effects of psilocybin usually start to be felt 20 to 40 minutes after ingestion, depending on the dose and one's metabolism.

Peak: This period typically happens 2 to 3 hours after intake, where the effects are most intense.

Come Down: 4 to 6 hours post-ingestion, the effects will gradually diminish.

Duration: Most psilocybin experiences last between 4 to 6 hours, though it might feel much longer due to an altered perception of time.

Sensory Changes

Visual: Vivid colors, geometric patterns, and visual hallucinations. Objects might appear to be breathing, and visual depth perception could change.

Auditory: Sounds might be heightened or distorted. Some report hearing music or sounds that aren't present.

Taste and smell: Both can be intensified.

Physical Sensations

Nausea: A common side effect, especially at the onset. It can be mitigated with fasting and dietary precautions.

Euphoria: Feelings of extreme happiness or joy.

Increased Heart Rate: Some may experience a faster heart rate.

Numbness: Especially in the face or extremities.

Muscle Weakness: This can feel like a heavy sensation in the limbs.

How to Cope With Common Side Effects

Nausea: As mentioned, fasting or eating light can help. Ginger or peppermint teas can also help soothe the stomach. If nausea persists, lying down and taking deep breaths can help. Avoid thinking about the nausea, as dwelling on it might amplify the feeling.

Anxiety: Creating a comfortable setting and ensuring you're in a safe environment can be reassuring. Deep breathing exercises and grounding techniques can be beneficial. If you're with someone, letting them know how you feel can help. Music can be a great tool to shift your mindset—have a playlist ready with calming and familiar songs.

Elevated Heart Rate: Avoid caffeine or any stimulants before the experience. Focusing on your breathing can help regulate your heart rate. If it persists and becomes uncomfortable, seek medical attention.

If the Experience Becomes Overwhelming:

- **Change the Setting:** Sometimes a simple change in environment, like moving to a quieter room or changing the music, can make a difference.
- **Grounding Techniques:** Touching or holding onto an object, focusing on your breath, or counting objects around you can help anchor you to reality.
- **Speak Up:** If you're with someone, let them know how you're feeling.
- **Remember It's Temporary:** Remembering that the experience will end and that you've taken a substance can help put things in perspective.
- **Seek Help:** If things become too intense, don't hesitate to seek medical attention.

While psilocybin has potential therapeutic benefits, its effects can vary widely among individuals. Proper preparation, understanding what to expect, and knowing how to cope with potential side effects are crucial for a safer, more controlled experience. Always prioritize safety and avoid self-medication without professional supervision.

Microdosing Psilocybin

When you think of psychedelic drugs, vivid and intense hallucinatory experiences might come to mind. However, in recent years, there's been a growing trend that diverges from the stereotypical use of these substances.

Microdosing, in the context of psychedelic substances, is the act of consuming a sub-perceptual amount. This means that, instead of taking the drug to "trip" or experience intense hallucinations, one takes a small fraction of that dose. For substances like psilocybin, derived from certain mushrooms, and LSD, this is often anywhere from 1/5 to 1/20 of a recreational dose.

The reasons people are drawn to microdosing are multifaceted. Anecdotal reports abound with individuals claiming enhancements in:

- Mood
- Creativity
- Concentration
- Productivity
- Empathy

However, the golden question remains: Is it the substance making the difference, or simply the expectation of a positive outcome (the expectancy effect)? The idea here is that if someone is told they're consuming something that will make them happier or more productive, merely believing this can result in those feelings, irrespective of what's actually consumed.

Calculating Microdose Levels

Given that potency can vary, especially with substances like psilocybin, which come from natural sources like mushrooms, calculating a consistent microdose can be tricky. Here's a rough guide:

Factor in Potency Variations

Understand that the potency can vary from one batch of mushrooms to another. This means the same weight from two different sources might yield different potencies.

Typical Microdose Ranges

Anecdotal evidence suggests a medium-strength dose of psilocybin mushrooms ranges from 2 to 3 grams of dried mushrooms. Therefore, a microdose might typically be around 0.3 grams (Grinspoon, 2022).

Regular Adjustments

Due to the risk of developing physiological tolerance, some users adjust their dose over time to maintain the same effect.

Source Verification

With the current state of legality and lack of regulation, it's vital to have a reliable supplier to ensure you're getting what you expect.

Two primary micro-dosing protocols have gained prominence:

Fadiman's Protocol

Developed by Dr. James Fadiman, this approach advises taking a microdose once every three days. This means dosing on Day 1, skipping days 2 and 3, and dosing again on day 4. The rationale is to experience the benefits on the day of dosing and the day after and then have a "break" before the next dose.

Stamets's Protocol

Paul Stamets, a renowned mycologist, suggests a more frequent schedule: microdosing daily for five days and then taking two days off.

Whichever method is chosen, individual variations will play a significant role. It's essential to start small, note the effects, and adjust as needed.

Safety Considerations and Potential Risks

One might think that due to the reduced dose, microdosing would inherently be safe. However, there are several concerns:

Long-Term Safety

The long-term impacts of microdosing remain unknown. There hasn't been sufficient research to say definitively if there are health risks associated with prolonged use.

Potential Overdose

Since the potency of substances like mushrooms can vary, there's a risk of inadvertently consuming a dose larger than intended.

Mental Health Implications

Individuals with significant mental illnesses, like schizophrenia or bipolar disorder, should be wary. While more research is needed, there are concerns about the potential risks of inducing or exacerbating symptoms.

Legal Risks

In many parts of the world, substances like psilocybin remain illegal, even in microdoses. Possession or use could result in legal penalties.

The world of microdosing psilocybin is as fascinating as it is mysterious. While anecdotes sing praises of its myriad benefits, science is still catching up in terms of understanding its safety and efficacy. As with any substance or treatment, it's crucial to approach microdosing with a blend of curiosity and caution, always prioritizing safety and well-being.

Mental Preparation

Embarking on a journey with microdosing, much like any profound life experience, requires thoughtful mental preparation. The key is not just to ingest a substance but to weave it into a holistic approach that encompasses intention, awareness, and mindset.

Setting an intention can be likened to planting a seed in the mind. This seed acts as your guide, ensuring that your experience has direction and purpose. When considering microdosing, ask yourself: What am I hoping to achieve? It could be clarity, a boost in creativity, or even seeking emotional tranquility. Once you've identified your "why," find ways to keep it front and center in your consciousness. Basic techniques, such as attaching a sticky note to your bathroom mirror or scheduling a daily alarm on your phone, act as stabilizers, guaranteeing that your intention stays clear and prominent. Journaling can be another powerful tool, allowing you to reflect and reaffirm your commitment to your chosen purpose.

Mindfulness

Microdosing, by its very nature, can magnify the internal dialogues and emotions within us. This heightened state can be both enlightening and overwhelming. This is where mindfulness steps in as a grounding force. By focusing on the present moment, whether it's the rhythm of your breath or the sensation of your fingers touching, you can navigate the experience with a clearer perspective. It's essential to remember that feelings, no matter how intense, are transient visitors. Greet them without judgment, understand their essence, and allow them to move on. Should emotions become particularly intense, revert to basic grounding techniques like concentrating on your breathing or the tactile sensation of your surroundings.

Cultivating a Positive and Supportive Mindset

As you begin this journey, fostering a supportive mindset is paramount. Anticipate and prepare for potential emotional upheavals. Recognize that, just like life, the microdosing journey might have its ups and downs. Prior to your experience, engage in activities that uplift your spirits and instill positivity. Whether it's listening to your favorite songs, spending time in nature, or engaging in a heartwarming conversation with a loved one, these activities can act as cushions, providing comfort during challenging times.

While the chemical compounds in psychedelics play a crucial role, the mental groundwork you lay is equally, if not more, essential. Approach microdosing with intention, awareness, and a well-nurtured mindset, and you're setting yourself up for a holistic and enriching experience.

Integration

Integration, then, becomes the bridge between these ephemeral insights and the tangible realm of our everyday lives. It's the process of internalizing, understanding, and applying the lessons and realizations we garner.

The Cornerstone of Integration

Imagine embarking on a profound journey and then returning home without unpacking your experiences. That's akin to engaging in microdosing without proper integration. The importance of integration lies in its ability to help us distill the essence of what we've learned and discovered about ourselves, making it integral for both personal growth and transformation. In essence, it's the act of taking those expansive, enlightening moments from microdosing and weaving them into the tapestry of our daily existence.

Reflection

One of the most potent tools in our integration toolkit is reflection. Journaling stands out as a particularly effective method. By putting pen to paper, you're externalizing your experiences, making them tangible. This not only solidifies your insights but also allows you to revisit and analyze them over time. The act of writing itself can sometimes unravel deeper layers of understanding that might initially escape conscious introspection.

But reflections don't always have to be solitary. Sharing your journey with supportive individuals can provide a fresh perspective. They might see things you missed or interpret your experiences in ways you hadn't considered. Their insights, combined with your own, can often form a more holistic picture.

For some, the abstract emotions and revelations from micro-dosing don't easily translate into words. Here, art and music step in. Crafting a piece of art or composing a melody based on your experience can offer a profound, non-verbal avenue of expression. This artistic endeavor doesn't demand perfection; it's the process and the emotions it evokes that hold value.

From Insights to Actions

True growth comes from not just experiencing revelations but also acting upon them. Begin by setting clear, actionable goals that align with your insights. If your journey revealed a yearning for stronger connections, perhaps your goal could be to spend more quality time with loved ones. Or if you felt a pull toward nature, maybe it's a commitment to weekly hikes.

However, change, even when driven by profound insights, can be daunting. It might necessitate breaking old habits, stepping out of comfort zones, or confronting long-standing fears. Support in such endeavors is invaluable. Whether it's seeking guidance from mentors, joining community groups with similar goals, or even professional therapy, surrounding yourself with a supportive network can make the transition smoother.

In summary, the beauty of a microdosing journey is not just in the moments of epiphany but in the lasting changes these moments can inspire. Integration is the alchemy that transforms these fleeting insights into enduring life changes. With reflection and proactive steps, one can ensure that the echoes of their psychedelic experiences resonate through the corridors of their daily life, leading to genuine transformation.

Chapter 9
The Future of Psilocybin and its Potential

In a quaint village nestled deep within the heart of the Amazon rainforest, an age-old ritual was taking place. Surrounded by the symphony of chirping crickets and distant owl hoots, a tribal shaman prepared a brew for a member of the community, aiming to heal the shadows of his soul. The main ingredient? Psilocybin. To the tribespeople, it was a sacred key that unlocked the door to inner transformation. But miles away, in bustling cities with skyscrapers touching the clouds, this humble mushroom ingredient was seen through a very different lens—often with skepticism, apprehension, or even outright fear.

Our journey with psilocybin often referred to as "magic mushrooms," is a testament to the complex relationship humanity has with psychoactive substances. Its story is inter-woven with tales of deep spiritual awakening on the one hand and decades of prohibition and stigma on the other. Fast forward to today, where scientists in pristine laboratories are unearthing the profound therapeutic potentials of psilocybin.

From providing solace to those trapped in the tight grip of depression and anxiety to offering hope to those battling the chains of addiction and PTSD, the tales of healing are becoming hard to ignore.

Yet, as with many tales of discovery, the path isn't straightforward. As we dive deep into the current research findings, we'll encounter controversies, breakthroughs, and glimpses of the sheer potential of this natural compound. How does modern society, with its intricate legal tapestries, reconcile with a substance that has been both venerated and vilified? The stark contrasts between its indigenous use and present-day laws challenge our perceptions and prompt us to question and introspect.

The winds of change, however, are beginning to blow. From the rain-soaked streets of Oregon to the sunny boulevards of Santa Cruz, the calls for decriminalization and legalization are getting louder. But as we edge closer to a potential new era of psilocybin acceptance, what does the future hold? Will we see it on the shelves of our pharmacies? As a staple in therapy sessions? Or perhaps as a catalyst for creative and spiritual quests?

Current Medical and Psychological Research Into Psilocybin

Magic mushrooms and their prime component, psilocybin, might still evoke images of tie-dyed T-shirts and Woodstock for many, but the past two decades have significantly altered our understanding of these natural substances. Far removed from their notorious association with the countercultural movements of the 60s, they are now becoming a beacon of hope in mental health research.

Psilocybin's Potential for Treating Mental Health Disorders

There is no denying the mounting evidence supporting psilo-cybin as a potentially revolutionary therapeutic tool. While currently deemed a Schedule I controlled substance, limiting broad-spectrum research, experts like Dr. Ryan Marino emphasize its evident safety when consumed in controlled environments.

Treatment-Resistant Depression, OCD, and Other Disorders

Consider its emerging role in addressing treatment-resistant depression. Findings from Johns Hopkins Medicine show that when paired with talk therapy, psilocybin can significantly ameliorate symptoms of clinical depression. Some partici-pants experienced lasting benefits, some even for an entire year, after just two doses. The implications? Psilocybin's ther-apeutic effects might not just be potent but enduring as well. This diverges from conventional treatments that often require daily, continual doses, hinting at a reduced risk of side effects with psilocybin.

Further, its therapeutic potential is not confined to depression alone. Promising outcomes have been observed in alleviating symptoms of obsessive-compulsive disorder and existential anxiety in terminally ill patients.

Smoking Cessation and Anorexia Nervosa

Beyond these domains, psilocybin is breaking new ground. Recent endeavors by institutions like Johns Hopkins, backed by federal funding, are unearthing its potential role in smoking cessation. Meanwhile, across the pond, COMPASS

Pathways in the UK has shared promising initial results on psilocybin's effects on patients with anorexia nervosa.

Decoding the "How" Behind Psilocybin's Effects

What makes psilocybin effective? Dive into the lived experiences of those who've undergone psilocybin therapy, and you'll frequently encounter narratives of profound, transformative "spiritual" experiences. Many report a heightened sense of "openness," encompassing increased sensitivity, creativity, and empathy.

This isn't just psychological rhetoric. This surge in openness post-psilocybin intake could be a byproduct of increased neuroplasticity. In layman's terms, psilocybin might be supercharging our brain's capacity to forge new connections, enhancing its adaptability. This potential ability to jolt the brain out of entrenched habits and debilitating thought patterns could be the secret behind its effectiveness against conditions like depression, anxiety, OCD, and addiction.

Psilocybin, Consciousness, and Creativity

Given the recurring theme of transformative experiences, it's no surprise that researchers are delving into psilocybin's impact on consciousness and creativity. The heightened sense of openness, a broadened perspective, and a richer emotional tapestry experienced by many can potentially unleash creative capacities previously dormant or constrained.

While the full spectrum of its effects on creativity remains an area ripe for investigation, anecdotal evidence and preliminary studies provide enough intrigue to warrant deeper exploration.

The Future

Microdosing, the practice of consuming tiny amounts of psilocybin, is another burgeoning area of interest. While anecdotal evidence speaks of its potential benefits for mental wellness, rigorous scientific scrutiny is essential before it becomes mainstream.

It's crucial to approach the psilocybin wave with informed enthusiasm. While its therapeutic potential is undeniable, it's not a free pass for unsupervised consumption. As Dr. Marino underscores, its consumption outside controlled settings carries risks. Adverse experiences, while reduced in controlled environments, can be detrimental when the substance is used recreationally or without appropriate guidance.

We stand on the cusp of what might be a seismic shift in mental health treatment paradigms. The psychedelic renaissance, with psilocybin at its helm, is challenging long-held beliefs, offering hope, and beckoning a future where mental health treatment is not just about symptom reduction but holistic transformation.

However, as with any nascent field, a fusion of enthusiasm with methodical research, stringent ethical guidelines, and public awareness is paramount. Psilocybin might indeed be a magic bullet for some of our most vexing mental health challenges, but like all magic, it requires a judicious, wise, and informed approach.

Overview of the Current Legal Landscape

The relationship between society and psychedelics, notably psilocybin, has long been complex. As research begins to shed light on their potential therapeutic benefits, laws across the globe are slowly evolving. But where does the world stand now, and what nuances surround the laws and their implications?

Current Laws Regarding Psilocybin

The United States

In 1973, psychedelics were classified as Schedule I substances, rendering them illegal. However, the winds of change started blowing in recent years, especially with states like Oregon taking steps toward legalizing the clinical use of psilocybin. Oregon's Psilocybin Services Act in 2020 mandated the state's health authority to regulate clinical psilocybin. Meanwhile, California has been leaning toward legalizing the possession, personal use, and sharing of psychedelics, with a bill passed by the Senate in 2021. Other cities like Denver, Oakland, Ann Arbor, and Cambridge have adopted similar stances.

Canada

While Canada hasn't been explicitly mentioned in the articles, it is noteworthy that they have begun to permit the use of psilocybin for end-of-life care. More expansive legislation or decriminalization initiatives are still in the works.

Europe

Europe's stance on psychedelics varies from country to country. Portugal stands out for its progressive drug policies, decriminalizing the use of all drugs, including psychedelics, in 2001. However, it is essential to differentiate between decriminalization and legalization.

Australia

This is not explicitly mentioned in the articles, but Australia's laws around psilocybin remain strict. It is classified as a Schedule 9 prohibited substance in the country.

The Legal Gray Areas and Consequences

There are various nuances surrounding psychedelic legalization. For instance, Oregon's approach seems to bet on the federal government turning a blind eye, much like with marijuana. However, the consequences of such discrepancies between state and federal law remain unclear.

A significant gray area lies in the use and accessibility of these substances. If commercialized, like cannabis, will it lead to overuse or misuse, especially without the needed therapeutic context? Violating these laws, given their Schedule I status, can lead to severe penalties, including incarceration. Yet, the exact implications differ from region to region, with some areas showing growing leniency while others remain stringent.

Contrast Between Traditional Indigenous Use and Modern Laws

Traditionally, many Indigenous cultures have revered psychedelics, using them in religious and spiritual ceremonies. These substances weren't just ingested; they were respected.

The modern legal landscape contrasts starkly. The potential therapeutic benefits of psilocybin are becoming more recognized, yet the substance remains illegal in many parts of the world.

Research has shown promise in treating conditions like depression, PTSD, and suicidality. However, concerns arise when distinguishing traditional ritual use from potential commercial use in a modern setting. The risks associated with psychedelics, especially when misused or used outside of a controlled, therapeutic environment, cannot be overlooked.

The global perspective on psilocybin is undergoing a transformation. While the promise of therapeutic benefits is tantalizing, a rush toward widespread legalization might be premature. Striking a balance between harnessing potential benefits, respecting traditional uses, and ensuring public safety remains the challenge for lawmakers worldwide. As with any substance, the key lies in education, understanding, and responsible implementation.

Decriminalization and Legalization Movements

In recent years, there's been a seismic shift in how societies view certain illicit substances, particularly psychedelics and cannabis. Once taboo, these substances are now at the forefront of robust discussions on decriminalization and legalization. This movement has gained traction primarily because of increased public awareness, rigorous scientific studies, and an evolving understanding of individual cognitive liberties. Let's dive deep into this phenomenon, particularly focusing on key locations like Oregon, Denver, Oakland, and Santa Cruz.

Overview of Recent Movements

Oregon

The Beaver State has always been at the forefront of progressive drug policies. Recently, it became the first U.S. state to decriminalize the possession of small amounts of all drugs, a radical move aiming to shift from criminalization to a health-centered approach. Additionally, in 2020, Oregonians voted to legalize psilocybin therapy, positioning psilocybin—the active compound in magic mushrooms—as a therapeutic tool under supervised settings.

Denver

Denver, Colorado, made headlines in May 2019 when it became the first U.S. city to decriminalize psilocybin. This was seen as a significant first step in the nationwide War on Drugs, moving the focus away from criminal penalties toward understanding and rehabilitation.

Oakland and Santa Cruz

Following Denver's lead, both Oakland and Santa Cruz, California decriminalized not only psilocybin but also other entheogenic plants and fungi, further pushing the envelope on the national discourse.

Arguments Made by These Movements

One of the primary drivers of these movements is the emerging research suggesting the medical benefits of these substances. Prestigious institutions like NYU, Johns Hopkins, and UCLA have found that substances like psilocybin can aid in treating depression, addiction, and other mental health issues.

Cognitive Liberty

This argument centers on the fundamental right of individuals to the conscious experience of their choosing, as long as it doesn't harm others. By this logic, prohibiting psychedelics infringes on personal cognitive freedom.

Religious Freedom

Entheogens, plants that contain psychoactive compounds, have been used in religious and spiritual rituals for centuries. The argument here is that prohibition restricts certain groups from practicing their religious beliefs fully.

Identity Politics and Neurodiversity

An emerging perspective likens "psychedelic identity" to other identity movements, like LGBTQ rights. The idea is that just as society has come to accept varying sexual orientations, it should also recognize and respect the neurodiverse experiences psychedelics provide.

Societal Implications

Decriminalizing these substances can help reduce the over-crowding of prisons with non-violent drug offenders and refocus law enforcement efforts on more pressing matters. Additionally, recognizing the therapeutic potential of these substances could revolutionize mental health care, potentially offering relief to millions.

Ways to Support Decriminalization and Legalization

Supporting the push toward decriminalization and legalization of certain substances, particularly psychedelics and cannabis, can be achieved through a multi-pronged approach.

Firstly, education stands as a paramount tool. By dispelling prevalent myths and disseminating accurate, research-based information about these substances, one can effectively shift public perception. Organizations and passionate individuals can take the lead by hosting workshops, seminars, webinars, and other informative events that offer a platform for experts to share their knowledge. The aim would be to enlighten the masses, ensuring that they are informed about the actual risks and benefits rather than being swayed by fear or misinformation.

Advocacy is another potent way to effect change. Grassroots movements, non-profit organizations, and individuals can work to directly influence policy by lobbying lawmakers, organizing public awareness campaigns, or even spearheading ballot measures in regions where citizens can directly propose laws. Connecting with local representatives, attending town hall meetings, and joining or organizing rallies can also amplify the voice of the movement.

One cannot underestimate the power of the ballot box. Voting remains one of the most direct ways individuals can influence policy. By researching and supporting candidates and initiatives that champion progressive drug policies, the public can help guide the trajectory of decriminalization and legalization in their regions. It's essential for voters to be well-informed and understand the implications of the policies they support.

Engaging in public discourse further extends the reach of the movement. Open conversations—whether they occur in traditional media, on social media platforms, through podcasts, or in day-to-day interactions—help dispel fears, challenge misconceptions, and normalize the discussion around these substances. Sharing personal experiences, where appropriate, can humanize the issue and make it more relatable.

Lastly, financial support can significantly accelerate the push toward more progressive drug policies. Research, advocacy, public campaigns, and even grassroots movements often require funding to make a tangible impact. By donating to or investing in organizations, research institutions, or campaigns that align with the decriminalization and legalization ethos, individuals can provide essential resources that propel the movement forward.

In essence, the road to decriminalization and legalization is paved with knowledge, active involvement, and collaboration. As society continues to evolve its stance on these substances, collective action will undoubtedly play a pivotal role in shaping the future.

The wave of decriminalization and legalization is not merely a cultural trend but a reflection of an evolving understanding of human consciousness, rights, and societal well-being. As we continue to grapple with these issues, it's crucial to approach them with an open mind, armed with knowledge and compassion. As history has shown, societal change often starts with challenging established norms, and this movement might just be the dawn of a new era in cognitive freedom and therapeutic potential.

The Future of Psilocybin in Medicine, Culture, and Personal Use

The reemergence of psychedelics, particularly psilocybin, into the limelight of contemporary medicine, popular culture, and personal exploration is like a phoenix rising from the ashes. Having been buried by societal fears, misinformation, and stigmatization, these compounds are now making a triumphant return. But as we traverse this new era, it's worth reflecting on their journey and speculating on their potential impact in various facets of our lives.

Shifting Attitudes on Understanding Psilocybin Over Time

The story of psilocybin, as with many psychedelics, can be likened to a roller-coaster. In the 1950s and 1960s, the psychiatric world viewed these compounds as potential wonder drugs, harbingers of revolutionary treatments for conditions like depression, anxiety, trauma, and addiction. Their promise was undeniable.

Yet, the tumultuousness of the counterculture movement, coupled with tales of harrowing trips and mental distress, led to a cloud of "moral panic" overshadowing these compounds. By the 1970s, they were largely vilified and banished from mainstream medicine and society. However, as the pendulum of time swings, so too do our perceptions. Recent studies and anecdotal reports are reigniting the spark of interest, and many are reconsidering psilocybin's value not just medically but culturally and personally.

Future Predictions

The recent medical literature is rich with studies showcasing the therapeutic potential of psilocybin. From treating major depressive disorder to alleviating the fears of terminally ill patients, this compound seems to have a broad spectrum of applications. The mechanism? It is a fascinating interplay of neuroscience and psyche. Dr. Jerrold Rosenbaum likens the action of psychedelics to "rebooting a computer" (Koellhoffer, n.d.). It seems that psilocybin, among others, can rewire entrenched neural circuits, allowing individuals to break free from rigid, debilitating patterns of thought and emotion. This "neuroplasticity" offers a potential key to treating many psychiatric ailments.

In future medicine, it's conceivable that we'll see specialized psychedelic therapeutic centers where controlled doses of psilocybin are administered under the supervision of trained professionals. These would be spaces where the mystical experiences catalyzed by psilocybin can be harnessed for healing, ensuring safety and maximizing therapeutic potential.

Potential Cultural and Societal Impacts of Wider Psilocybin Acceptance and Use

Beyond the realm of medicine, the cultural and societal implications of embracing psilocybin are profound. Historically, many Indigenous cultures have revered psychedelic substances, integrating them into rituals and spiritual practices. As modern society begins to recognize the depth of experience these compounds can offer, we might see a revival of these ancient practices, perhaps tailored to our contemporary needs.

As with any powerful tool, there's the risk of misuse. The euphoric states induced by substances like MDMA might tempt some to recreational excess, leading to potential physical and psychological harm. Thus, as a society, we must walk this path with a mix of enthusiasm and caution.

Role of Individual Responsibility and Education

The future of psilocybin largely hinges on two things: individual responsibility and education. While the allure of a transformative experience might be enticing, it's crucial to remember that these are potent compounds. Using them without proper guidance or in inappropriate settings can have adverse outcomes.

Education plays a pivotal role here. As we stand at the cusp of a psychedelic renaissance, it's essential to disseminate accurate information about the benefits and risks of psilocybin. Workshops, seminars, and even school curricula can incorporate information on safe use, helping to demystify these substances and minimize potential harm.

The narrative of psilocybin is still being written. Its journey from ancient ritual to modern medicine, from vilification to redemption, serves as a testament to humanity's evolving relationship with nature and consciousness. With prudence, curiosity, and a commitment to understanding, we stand to unlock a treasure trove of therapeutic, cultural, and personal insights. The future, it seems, is indeed psychedelic.

Conclusion

The odyssey into the world of psilocybin mushrooms is both mesmerizing and transformative. But as with all journeys of great depth and potential, it demands respect, understanding, and responsibility. These mushrooms, brimming with ancient wisdom and powerful effects, open doors to realms previously uncharted for many. But like all doors, some lead to enlightenment, while others to challenge, making it imperative to tread with knowledge and care.

When we speak of safety, it's not a mere afterthought—it's foundational. Psilocybin's effects span the spectrum from deeply transcendental to profoundly challenging. Every person embarking on this journey should be intimately familiar with what lies ahead, preparing both mind and body. It's crucial to recognize the potential side effects and navigate them with grace. From the fleeting anxiety that may cloud one's mind to the physical sensations like nausea that can sometimes accompany a trip, understanding these aspects is paramount.

Conclusion

But our responsibilities don't end with understanding the physiological implications. The global tapestry of psilocybin legality is a labyrinthine one, stitched together by myriad socio-cultural, historical, and political threads. In some corners of the world, a dance with these fungi is a legally sanctioned rite, while in others, it can mean punitive repercussions. Every individual who feels the call of psilocybin owes it to themselves and their communities to be well-versed in the local legal statutes. Ignorance, after all, isn't just a personal risk—it's a communal one.

As humanity has evolved, so has its relationship with consciousness-altering substances. Historically, these relationships have oscillated between reverence and recklessness. With psilocybin, we find ourselves at a crossroads with the potential to etch a future rooted in respect and understanding. Knowledge, in this realm, is both a shield and a compass. Proper dosage, understanding the profound influence of "set and setting," and integrating the experience into one's life are pillars of responsible use. As guardians of our own minds and bodies, it's our duty to adhere to these principles, ensuring that our experiences remain enlightening and never perilous.

Yet, our era—one of unprecedented access to information—presents its own challenges. While a wealth of knowledge is at our fingertips, so too is a deluge of misinformation. It becomes an act of discernment to separate the chaff from the grain. Hence, a commitment to rigorous inquiry, a deep dive into scientific literature, consultation with reputable sources, and engagement with professionals in the field is non-negotiable. The realm of psilocybin is not one for armchair experts —it demands genuine scholarship and responsible knowledge dissemination.

Conclusion

The transformative power of psilocybin doesn't merely end with personal revelations; it extends to a broader societal canvas. Those who have been touched by its magic become ambassadors for a brighter future—a world where harm reduction practices are universal, and where legal landscapes shift to reflect our deeper understanding of these ancient organisms.

And as we come full circle in our exploration, let's once again bask in the awe of the fungal kingdom. These organisms, often hidden in plain sight, are Earth's silent nurturers, the unseen connectors of life. The psilocybin mushroom, with its unique blend of chemicals, offers more than just a trip—it provides a paradigm shift.

Mycology beckons us to reflect on larger themes: the wondrous interconnections of nature, the intricacies of consciousness, and the untapped reservoirs of healing nestled within the planet. These fungi are both teachers and healers, guiding those who seek their wisdom on a path of discovery, transformation, and growth.

To engage with psilocybin mushrooms—whether by cultivation, consumption, or mere academic curiosity—is to participate in an age-old dance of nature and consciousness. It is an invitation to both personal and societal evolution. In these fungi, we glimpse not only the profound mysteries of nature but also the boundless potential of the human spirit.

As we wrap up this exploration, the call to action is clear: Arm oneself with knowledge, approach with reverence, and tread with responsibility. Psilocybin mushrooms offer a world of wonder, waiting to be understood and respected. And for those who heed this call, the journey promises to be as transformative as the destination.

Don't Miss Out: Your Exclusive Guide Awaits!

As you turn the final pages of "The Magic of Mycology," the journey doesn't have to end here. Elevate your cultivation practice by claiming your complimentary copy of "Psilocybin Simplified: A Rapid Guide to Mushroom Cultivation and Microdose Capsule Making."

Why You Should Download "Psilocybin Simplified":

- **Direct, Practical Steps**: Discover clear, concise instructions for growing psilocybin mushrooms and crafting microdose capsules.
- **Unlock Expert Techniques**: Benefit from advanced tips and strategies to enhance your cultivation skills.
- **Access Exclusive Offers**: Gain special access to discounts and offers on spores and cultivation supplies, curated just for our readers.

Secure Your Free Guide Now!

Conclusion

To download your free copy of "Psilocybin Simplified," simply visit magicofmycology.com and provide your email. Take advantage of this opportunity to access a wealth of knowledge and exclusive offers to support your mycological endeavors.

We're excited to support your continued exploration of psilocybin mushrooms. Grab your guide today and take the next step in mastering the art of mushroom cultivation.

I Hope You Enjoyed Our Journey Together!

Thank you for exploring "The Magic of Mycology: An Enthusiast's Guide to Cultivating and Understanding Psilocybin Mushrooms" with me. It has been a privilege to share my passion and knowledge with you, and I hope your journey through the pages has been as enlightening and enriching as the fascinating world of psilocybin mushrooms.

If this book has inspired you, sparked your curiosity, or deepened your understanding of mycology, I would be deeply grateful if you could take a moment to share your experience.

Why Your Review Matters:

- **Support Our Growing Community**: Your feedback not only helps others discover the magic of mycology but also strengthens our community of enthusiasts.
- **Share Your Unique Insights**: Your perspective is invaluable, and sharing it can enlighten others and enrich the collective conversation around psilocybin mushrooms.

- **Inspire Continued Exploration**: Your thoughts encourage me and others to delve deeper into the mysteries and wonders of mycology.

How You Can Leave a Review:

Leaving a review is simple:

- Visit the platform where you purchased or accessed the book.
- Look for the option to write a review.
- Share your journey, insights, and the impact "The Magic of Mycology" has had on you.

Every review and insight you share makes a profound difference. It's not just about supporting me; it's about nurturing a passionate, informed, and curious mycology community.

Thank you for your time, your curiosity, and your willingness to embark on this mycological adventure with me. I'm eagerly looking forward to hearing about your journey!

References

Alexander, S. (2023, May 15). *A guide to manure-loving mushrooms.* Shroomer. https://www.shroomer.com/guide-to-coprophilous-fungi/

Bach, D., Burk, J., Kirkendall, A., & Lenihan, J. (2013). *The rise and fall of the American counterculture: A history of hippies and other cultural dissidents.* https://oaktrust.library.tamu.edu/bitstream/handle/1969.1/151736/BACH-DISSERTATION-2013.pdf?sequence=1&isAllowed=n

Beyer, D. M. (2022, October 21). *Six steps to mushroom farming.* Penn State Extension. https://extension.psu.edu/six-steps-to-mushroom-farming

Brainstem: overview, function & anatomy. (2021, June 21). Cleveland Clinic. https://my.clevelandclinic.org/health/body/21598-brainstem

Cherry, K. (2020, June 16). *The Location and Function of the Cerebellum in the Brain.* Verywell Mind. https://www.verywellmind.com/what-is-the-cerebellum-2794964#:~:text=The%20cerebellum%20(which%20is%20Latin

Frontal Lobe: what it is, function, location & damage. (2022). Cleveland Clinic. https://my.clevelandclinic.org/health/body/24501-frontal-lobe

Fungus — reproductive processes of fungi. (2019). Encyclopædia Britannica. https://www.britannica.com/science/fungus/Reproductive-processes-of-fungi

Garcia de Teresa, M. (2022). *Selling the priceless mushroom: A history of Psilocybin mushroom trade in the sierra mazateca* (Oaxaca). *Journal of Illicit Economies and Development,* *4*(2), 177–190. https://doi.org/10.31389/jied.101

Grinspoon, P. (2022, September 19). *The popularity of microdosing of psychedelics: What does the science say?* Harvard Health. https://www.health.harvard.edu/blog/the-popularity-of-microdosing-of-psychedelics-what-does-the-science-say-202209192819

Hoa, H. T., & Wang, C.-L. (2015). *The effects of temperature and nutritional conditions on mycelium growth of two oyster mushrooms* (Pleurotus ostreatus and Pleurotus cystidiosus). *Mycobiology,* *43*(1), 14–23. https://doi.org/10.5941/myco.2015.43.1.14

Jay. (2020, November 17). *The easy guide on how to identify magic mushrooms.* Mushroom Site. https://mushroomsite.com/2020/11/17/how-to-identify-magic-mushrooms/

References

Koellhoffer, T. (n.d.). *Ecstasy and other club drugs* - PDF Free Download. Epdf.pub. https://epdf.pub/ecstasy-and-other-club-drugs.html

Ly, C., Greb, A. C., Cameron, L. P., Wong, J. M., Barragan, E. V., Wilson, P. C., Burbach, K. F., Soltanzadeh Zarandi, S., Sood, A., Paddy, M. R., Duim, W. C., Dennis, M. Y., McAllister, A. K., Ori-McKenney, K. M., Gray, J. A., & Olson, D. E. (2018). Psychedelics promote structural and functional neural plasticity. *Cell Reports*, *23*(11), 3170–3182. https://doi.org/10.1016/j.celrep.2018.05.022

Mitra, S., Prova, S. R., Sultana, S. A., Das, R., Nainu, F., Emran, T. B., Tareq, A. M., Uddin, Md. S., Alqahtani, A. M., Dhama, K., & Simal-Gandara, J. (2021). Therapeutic potential of indole alkaloids in respiratory diseases: A comprehensive review. *Phytomedicine*, *90*, 153649. https://doi.org/10.1016/j.phymed.2021.153649

Oana-Mihaela, G. (n.d.). *Plants of the Gods*. Academia. https://www.academia.edu/44946736/PLANTS_OF_THE_GODS

Partridge, C. (2018). *Psychedelic shamanism*. Oxford University Press eBooks. https://doi.org/10.1093/oso/9780190459116.003.0009

Strauss, D., Ghosh, S., Murray, Z., & Marieka Gryzenhout. (2023). Global species diversity and distribution of the psychedelic fungal genus Panaeolus. *Heliyon*, *9*(6), e16338–e16338. https://doi.org/10.1016/j.heliyon.2023.e16338

Terry, N., & Margolis, K. G. (2017). Serotonergic mechanisms regulating the GI tract: experimental evidence and therapeutic relevance. *Handbook of Experimental Pharmacology*, 239, 319–342. https://doi.org/10.1007/164_2016_103

Winkelman, M. J. (2021). *The evolved psychology of psychedelic set and setting: inferences regarding the roles of shamanism and entheogenic ecopsychology. Frontiers in Pharmacology*, 12. https://doi.org/10.3389/fphar.2021.619890

Witt, E. (2018, May 29). *The psychedelic renaissance: trip reports from Timothy Leary, Michael Pollan, and Tao Lin*. The New Yorker. https://www.newyorker.com/books/under-review/the-science-of-the-psychedelic-renaissance